JULIA MORGAN

JULIA MORGAN

CARY JAMES

CHELSEA HOUSE PUBLISHERS

NEW YORK • PHILADELPHIA

Chelsea House Publishers
EDITOR-IN-CHIEF Nancy Toff
EXECUTIVE EDITOR Remmel T. Nunn
MANAGING EDITOR Karyn Gullen Browne
COPY CHIEF Juliann Barbato
PICTURE EDITOR Adrian G. Allen
ART DIRECTOR Maria Epes
MANUFACTURING MANAGER Gerald Levine

American Women of Achievement
SENIOR EDITOR Richard Rennert

Staff for JULIA MORGAN
TEXT EDITOR Constance Jones
COPY EDITOR Karen Hammonds
EDITORIAL ASSISTANT Nicole Claro
PICTURE RESEARCHER Patricia Burns
ASSISTANT ART DIRECTOR Loraine Machlin
DESIGNER Debora Smith
LAYOUT Kathe Burkhart
PRODUCTION MANAGER Joseph Romano
PRODUCTION COORDINATOR Marie Claire Cebrián
COVER ART David Dircks

3 5 7 9 8 6 4

Library of Congress Cataloging-in-Publicaton Data

James, Cary, 1935–
  Julia Morgan.
  (American women of achievement)
  Bibliography: p.
  Includes index.
  1. Morgan, Julia, 1872–1957. 2. Architects—
California—Biography. 3. Architecture, Modern—20th
century—California. 4. Architecture—California.
I. Title. II. Series.
NA737.M68J36 1988   720'.92'4 [B]   87-25615
ISBN 1-55546-669-9
     0-7910-0445-7

CONTENTS

AMERICAN WOMEN OF ACHIEVEMENT

Abigail Adams
women's rights advocate

Jane Addams
social worker

Louisa May Alcott
author

Marian Anderson
singer

Susan B. Anthony
woman suffragist

Ethel Barrymore
actress

Clara Barton
*founder of the American
Red Cross*

Elizabeth Blackwell
physician

Nellie Bly
journalist

Margaret Bourke-White
photographer

Pearl Buck
author

Rachel Carson
biologist and author

Mary Cassatt
artist

Agnes de Mille
choreographer

Emily Dickinson
poet

Isadora Duncan
dancer

Amelia Earhart
aviator

Mary Baker Eddy
*founder of the Christian
Science church*

Betty Friedan
feminist

Althea Gibson
tennis champion

Emma Goldman
political activist

Helen Hayes
actress

Lillian Hellman
playwright

Katharine Hepburn
actress

Karen Horney
psychoanalyst

Anne Hutchinson
religious leader

Mahalia Jackson
gospel singer

Helen Keller
humanitarian

Jeane Kirkpatrick
diplomat

Emma Lazarus
poet

Clare Boothe Luce
author and diplomat

Barbara McClintock
biologist

Margaret Mead
anthropologist

Edna St. Vincent Millay
poet

Julia Morgan
architect

Grandma Moses
painter

Louise Nevelson
sculptor

Sandra Day O'Connor
Supreme Court justice

Georgia O'Keeffe
painter

Eleanor Roosevelt
diplomat and humanitarian

Wilma Rudolph
champion athlete

Florence Sabin
medical researcher

Beverly Sills
opera singer

Gertrude Stein
author

Gloria Steinem
feminist

Harriet Beecher Stowe
author and abolitionist

Mae West
entertainer

Edith Wharton
author

Phillis Wheatley
poet

Babe Didrikson Zaharias
champion athlete

CHELSEA HOUSE PUBLISHERS

"REMEMBER THE LADIES"

MATINA S. HORNER

Remember the Ladies." That is what Abigail Adams wrote to her husband, John, then a delegate to the Continental Congress, as the Founding Fathers met in Philadelphia to form a new nation in March of 1776. "Be more generous and favorable to them than your ancestors. Do not put such unlimited power in the hands of the Husbands. If particular care and attention is not paid to the Ladies," Abigail Adams warned, "we are determined to foment a Rebellion, and will not hold ourselves bound by any Laws in which we have no voice, or Representation."

The words of Abigail Adams, one of the earliest American advocates of women's rights, were prophetic. Because when we have not "remembered the ladies," they have, by their words and deeds, reminded us so forcefully of the omission that we cannot fail to remember them. For the history of American women is as interesting and varied as the history of our nation as a whole. American women have played an integral part in founding, settling, and building our country. Some we remember as remarkable women who—against great odds—achieved distinction in the public arena: Anne Hutchinson, who in the 17th century became a charismatic religious leader; Phillis Wheatley, an 18th-century black slave who became a poet; Susan B. Anthony, whose name is synonymous with the 19th-century women's rights movement and who led the struggle to enfranchise women; and, in our own century, Amelia Earhart, the first woman to cross the Atlantic Ocean by air.

These extraordinary women certainly merit our admiration, but other women, "common women," many of them all but forgotten, should also be recognized for their contributions to American thought and culture. Women have been community builders; they have founded schools and formed voluntary associations to help those in need; they have assumed the major responsibility for rearing children, passing on from one generation to the next the values that keep a culture alive. These and innumerable other contributions, once ignored, are now being recognized by scholars, students, and the public. It is exciting and gratifying to realize that a part of our history that was hardly acknowledged a few generations ago is now being studied and brought to light.

In recent decades, the field of women's history has grown from obscurity to a politically controversial splinter movement to academic respectability, in many cases mainstreamed into such traditional disciplines as history, economics, and psychology. Scholars of women, both female and male, have organized research centers at such prestigious institutions as Wellesley College, Stanford University, and the University of California. Other notable centers for women's studies are the Center for the American Woman and Politics at the Eagleton Institute of Politics at Rutgers University; the Henry A. Murray Research Center for the Study of Lives, at Radcliffe College; and the Women's Research and Education Institute, the research arm of the Congressional Caucus on Women's Issues. Other scholars and public figures have established archives and libraries, such as the Schlesinger Library on the History of Women in America, at Radcliffe College, and the Sophia Smith Collection, at Smith College, to collect and preserve the written and tangible legacies of women.

From the initial donation of the Women's Rights Collection in 1943, the Schlesinger Library grew to encompass vast collections documenting the manifold accomplishments of American women. Simultaneously, the women's movement in general and the academic discipline of women's studies in particular also began with a narrow definition and gradually expanded their mandate. Early causes such as woman suffrage and social reform, abolition and organized labor were joined by newer concerns such as the history of women in business and the professions and in politics and government; the study of the family; and social issues such as health policy and education.

Women, as historian Arthur M. Schlesinger, jr., once pointed out, "have constituted the most spectacular casualty of traditional history.

They have made up at least half the human race, but you could never tell that by looking at the books historians write." The new breed of historians is remedying that omission. They have written books about immigrant women and about working-class women who struggled for survival in cities and about black women who met the challenges of life in rural areas. They are telling the stories of women who, despite the barriers of tradition and economics, became lawyers and doctors and public figures.

The women's studies movement has also led scholars to question traditional interpretations of their respective disciplines. For example, the study of war has traditionally been an exercise in military and political analysis, an examination of strategies planned and executed by men. But scholars of women's history have pointed out that wars have also been periods of tremendous change and even opportunity for women, because the very absence of men on the home front enabled them to expand their educational, economic, and professional activities and to assume leadership in their homes.

The early scholars of women's history showed a unique brand of courage in choosing to investigate new subjects and take new approaches to old ones. Often, like their subjects, they endured criticism and even ostracism by their academic colleagues. But their efforts have unquestionably been worthwhile, because with the publication of each new study and book another piece of the historical patchwork is sewn into place, revealing an increasingly comprehensive picture of the role of women in our rich and varied history.

Such books on groups of women are essential, but books that focus on the lives of individuals are equally indispensable. Biographies can be inspirational, offering their readers the example of people with vision who have looked outside themselves for their goals and have often struggled against great obstacles to achieve them. Marian Anderson, for instance, had to overcome racial bigotry in order to perfect her art and perform as a concert singer. Isadora Duncan defied the rules of classical dance to find true artistic freedom. Jane Addams had to break down society's notions of the proper role for women in order to create new social institutions, notably the settlement house. All of these women had to come to terms both with themselves and with the world in which they lived. Only then could they move ahead as pioneers in their chosen callings.

Biography can inspire not only by adulation but also by realism. It helps us to see not only the qualities in others that we hope to emulate but also, perhaps, the weaknesses that made them "human." By helping us identify with the subject on a more personal level they help us to feel that we, too, can achieve such goals. We read about Eleanor Roosevelt, for example, who occupied a unique and seemingly enviable position as the wife of the president. Yet we can sympathize with her inner dilemma: an inherently shy woman who had to force herself to live a most public life in order to use her position to benefit others. We may not be able to imagine ourselves having the immense poetic talent of Emily Dickinson, but from her story we can understand the challenges faced by a creative woman who was expected to fulfill many family responsibilities. And though few of us will ever reach the level of athletic accomplishment displayed by Wilma Rudolph or Babe Zaharias, we can still appreciate their spirit, their overwhelming will to excel.

A biography is a multifaceted lens. It is first of all a magnification, the intimate examination of one particular life. But at the same time, it is a wide-angle lens, informing us about the world in which the subject lived. We come away from reading about one life knowing more about the social, political, and economic fabric of the time. It is for this reason, perhaps, that the great New England essayist Ralph Waldo Emerson wrote, in 1841, "There is properly no history: only biography." And it is also why biography, and particularly women's biography, will continue to fascinate writers and readers alike.

JULIA MORGAN

In 1904, Julia Morgan became the first woman in California to receive an architect's license. Two years later, at the age of 34, she renovated the earthquake-twisted Fairmont Hotel and embarked on a long and successful career.

ONE

Rising from the Ashes

On April 18, 1906, a Wednesday, the glowing sky promised a clear dawn and a beautiful day. Julia Morgan was sleeping soundly in an upstairs bedroom when, at 5:16 A.M., the continent west of California's San Andreas fault jerked northward. The greatest movement—more than 20 feet—occurred 30 miles north of San Francisco. Throughout the San Francisco Bay area, streets fractured and buildings crumbled.

The earthquake lasted 40 seconds. A man in Berkeley woke ". . . to find the house shaking, amid violent creaking and cracking, so loud as to drown out the crash of falling chimneys. Recognizing that it was an earthquake, one expected it to cease every moment, but after a movement of less violence, the horrible shaking began again, with greater intensity, until it seemed the house must collapse bodily."

In Oakland, the Morgan house creaked and groaned. Light fixtures swung from the ceilings and dishes toppled from kitchen cabinets. Julia Morgan was jolted awake by the frightening motion, unaware that this catastrophe would have a profound effect on her budding career.

The quake shattered scores of windows in downtown Oakland. Brick buildings fell into the streets, and the corner tower of the First Baptist Church collapsed, along with the walls of its peaked gables. At nearby Mills College one of the classroom buildings crumbled, but the new library and the bell tower, both completed recently, stood without a crack. Julia Morgan, who in 1904 had become the first woman registered as an architect by the state of California, had designed and supervised the construction of both structures.

In the unnerving silence that followed the initial shock of the earthquake, Morgan prepared to go across the bay to San Francisco, where she had opened her own office just months earlier. San Francisco was closer to the center of the earthquake and had suffered much greater damage. Brick chimneys had collapsed everywhere, and poorly built rooming houses and small hotels lay warped and shattered.

In the wholesale market district, brick warehouse fronts had toppled into the streets, killing people and horses. Downtown, the new city hall was in shambles.

But worse than that, the quake had severed gas pipes and knocked over burning oil heaters. Fires broke out almost immediately, and by six o'clock in the morning a dozen city blocks were burning. At seven, when Morgan boarded her ferry, the skyline of San Francisco was obscured by towering columns of smoke. To Morgan, worried about her office and about her staff, the ride seemed endless.

By the time she landed, a mile of wooden buildings was in flames south of Market Street, the city's main thoroughfare. Rolling smoke blotted out the sun. Morgan had to walk the six blocks to her office in the new Merchants' Exchange Building, through the glass and rubble that filled the streets. In the business district north of Market Street, most of the structures were of brick or concrete, supposedly fireproof. But Morgan knew that, even if the buildings themselves would not burn, everything inside could easily catch fire. On the way to her office she passed several small blazes that unless they were stopped would move relentlessly from one building to the next.

At the Merchants' Exchange the electricity had failed. The elevators did not work, and the stairs were dark and dangerous. After the long climb to her ruined office, Morgan could only stare out at the city through broken windows. She could do no work and so climbed down again. A few people

After the tremors of the 1906 quake stopped, fire swept through a shattered San Francisco and troops patroled the streets to prevent looting.

San Franciscans view earthquake destruction along California Street, with the Merchants' Exchange building, site of Morgan's office, in the distance.

walked through the wrecked streets or stood watching the fires. On her way back to the ferry she passed small fire companies struggling against the obstinate flames and saw armed soldiers, called out by the mayor to guard against looting. That afternoon the Merchants' Exchange Building caught fire. It burned all through the night, and on Thursday morning only its outside walls stood amid the surrounding rubble.

San Francisco, the city that had grown with such abandon after the frenzy of the 1849 gold rush, burned for four days. By Saturday evening, when a light rain finally dampened the ashes,

490 city blocks lay blackened and smoking. More than a thousand people had died. One observer wrote: "A very few people were to be seen among the ruins, which added much to the general gloom of the situation. I found it difficult then, and ever since, very difficult to locate myself when wandering in the ruined district, as all the old landmarks are gone."

At the summit of Nob Hill, where the ornate Stanford and Hopkins mansions had been reduced to rubble, the Fairmont Hotel, newly completed and quite luxurious, wore an eyebrow of soot over every burned-out window. Much of the hotel was still sound, but

15

The 1906 earthquake demolished entire districts, leaving thousands of families homeless. Refugees tried to carry on as usual despite the catastrophe.

The Fairmont Hotel (top right) was one of the few Nob Hill buildings left standing after the cataclysm. A fire from the earthquake, however, had warped its structure and gutted its interior.

the earthquake had caused the structure to buckle. The Fairmont needed major repairs. According to one account, the owners asked Stanford White, a famous New York architect, to take charge of the rebuilding. But White, an untiring ladies' man, was shot by a jealous husband before he could begin the job.

The owners of the Fairmont ultimately assigned the job of restoring the hotel to Julia Morgan, then only 34. It was, in retrospect, quite a remarkable choice. At the time, virtually all practicing architects and contractors were men. But California was more progressive than many other states. As a booming frontier region, the state fostered individualism and independence. Although California would not grant women suffrage—the right to vote—until 1911, its suffrage laws would be on the books for nine years before women would win that right nationally.

For her part, Julia Morgan had consistently refused to accept society's limitations on women. As a teenager, she had decided that she wanted a career even though it was expected that most women of her class, if they finished high school at all, would marry quickly and become wives and mothers. But with the encouragement and support of her parents, Julia Morgan had decided instead to become an ar-

17

chitect. She was the first woman to graduate with a civil engineering degree from the University of California at Berkeley (which did not yet have an architecture program).

Armed with her degree, Julia Morgan had then taken another unprecedented step. At the age of 24 she had traveled to Paris to seek admission to the most famous architecture school in the world, the École des Beaux-Arts (School of Fine Arts)—which did not accept women students at that time. Morgan had nevertheless spent two years preparing herself and taking difficult entrance examinations. Finally, in 1898, she had become the first woman ever admitted to the school's architecture section, and at the age of 30, she received her Certificat in architecture, the first woman ever to do so.

Now, four years later, Morgan faced another challenge: the reconstruction of the Fairmont Hotel. She had already done excellent work elsewhere, including at Mills College, and those structures withstood the earthquake. She was determined that her work on the Fairmont would be equally solid.

To tackle this large and complex job, she formed a partnership with Ira Hoover, a friend from a firm that had employed her when she first returned from Paris. Morgan and Hoover found temporary office space in Oakland while they waited for the Merchants' Exchange to be rebuilt. They would work together for four years, until Hoover returned to the East Coast.

After attaining the Fairmont commission, Morgan spent weeks clambering through the blackened hotel interior, checking the fire damage. A small, slender woman just over five feet tall, she tramped across the high roofs and peered down through large holes where skylights had collapsed. Her job was to direct the replacement of structural beams and columns.

When Morgan had received her Certificat from Beaux-Arts, her *patron* (tutor) had predicted that she would have to restrict her activities to design and thus do all her work in the office. He thought she would make a good architect, but he said that a proper young lady would not be able to inspect buildings under construction—the work was too hazardous. Morgan refused to be limited in this manner, but she had at least one obstacle to overcome.

At that time, ladies' fashions stressed leisure and gentility, with high collars, long sleeves, and skirts nearly to the ground. But Morgan, a practicing architect, had to walk through buildings littered with construction materials, climb rickety ladders, and cross high scaffolding, and conventional women's clothing made this awkward. She found a solution: On building sites she wore a pair of men's trousers under her long skirts. In less demanding situations, she usually wore a trim, dark jacket, a white blouse, and a long, conservative skirt. Beneath her close-fitting hat she pulled her wavy hair into a neat bun, and horn-rimmed glasses framed her dark eyes. She never failed to convey an air of authority.

Learning that a woman was in charge of rebuilding San Francisco's newest

Morgan's associates work in makeshift quarters. Her offices destroyed, Morgan moved her practice to Oakland and formed a partnership with Ira Hoover.

hotel, a local reporter tracked her down amid the scaffolding and the clutter. She described Morgan as "a small, slender young woman with something Quakerish about her." The reporter, who assumed that Morgan was the decorator in charge of such tasks as repainting the walls, gushed, "How you must have reveled in this chance to squeeze dry the loveliest tubes in the whole world of color!"

Morgan turned to the reporter with a wry smile and remarked: "I don't think you understand just what my work here has been. The decorative part was all done by a New York firm. In fact, most of it was finished before the fire and has been restored on the same lines and in the same tones. My work has been all structural." That interview is thought to be the only one Morgan ever gave. The architect appeared to court "obscurity," as one writer put it. She believed that her buildings, representing the best possible work, should speak for her, and that, as biographer Sara Boutelle noted, "architecture was a visual, not a verbal art."

The Fairmont Hotel required extensive renovations after the 1906 earthquake, as this view of the sixth floor corridor shows. Morgan's engineering education proved invaluable in the completion of her first major project.

When Morgan completed her structural work on the Fairmont, other architects and designers supervised the refinishing of the hotel's interior.

Even before the Fairmont project, Morgan had insisted on quality construction. She was known for her strict personal supervision of every phase of a project. On one occasion, the brickwork of a house chimney did not satisfy her and she began to demolish it with her bare hands. An employee remembered that "she never raised her voice or got angry, but . . . she was very insistent on the work being done correctly and properly. . . . She followed up everything on the work in the field."

On the Fairmont job, as on all her others, Morgan quickly earned the re-spect of the builders. Asked about working for a woman, the foreman replied gruffly: "An architect's an architect, and you can count them all on the fingers of one hand. Now this building is in [the] charge of a real architect and her name happens to be Julia Morgan."

Her work on the hotel also generated a great deal of publicity for Morgan, and it established once and for all her reputation as an architect of the first order. Out of the ruins of earthquake-shattered San Francisco, Julia Morgan built for herself a rewarding—and highly praised—career.

Julia Morgan, shown here at about age eight, enjoyed a comfortable childhood in Oakland, California, across the bay from booming San Francisco.

T W O

California Dreaming

Julia Morgan grew up in Oakland, California, on the eastern edge of the San Francisco Bay. The city had started out in the 1840s, 25 years before Morgan's birth, as a few small towns scattered across level bay-shore lands. For many years California had remained isolated and thinly populated, when, after a century of Mexican rule, it became a territory of the United States in 1848. That year gold was discovered at John Sutter's sawmill a few miles away. For a dozen years California was mad with "gold fever," and the area's population increased rapidly.

The state had other attractions as well, such as a good climate and rich farming lands. Even after the excitement of the gold rush had faded, people continued to pour into California. In 1869 the railroad linked the state to Chicago and the East Coast. But whereas San Francisco retained its brawling gold-rush image for many years, Oakland soon became a sedate city filled with homes and churches.

Julia Morgan's parents, Charles Bill Morgan and Eliza Parmalee Morgan, came west from New York City soon after the completion of the railroad. Bill Morgan was a small, well-dressed man, outgoing and full of laughter. Eliza, the daughter of A. O. Parmalee, a wealthy cotton trader, was quieter and more pensive.

When they first arrived, the Morgans stayed at the Palace Hotel, San Francisco's finest. Bill Morgan had planned to become a sugar broker in Hawaii, but the Morgans found California to their liking and decided to settle there. They rented a house in San Francisco where Parmalee, their first son, was born. Julia followed, on January 26, 1872. The other children, Emma, Avery, and Gardiner, were born after the family moved across the bay.

In about 1872 Bill Morgan bought a building lot in Oakland, at the corner of 14th and Brush streets, then the city's northern boundary. He built a comfortable home, clad in wood siding and decorative shingles and ornamented in the Victorian style. Julia grew up in that house. The front hall, lined with wood paneling, was always dim and cool on summer days, and the large front parlor and the dining room were filled with potted plants, thick curtains, and heavy, ornate furniture. On the second floor, Julia shared a large room with her sister, Emma, who was two years younger than she. The upper story of the Morgan house had rooms for the maid and the cook, where the ceilings sloped and the windows peeked through the triangular gables of the roof.

The house's bay windows were Julia's special place. From them, she could look out through the elm trees planted recently along the street. Beyond the wooden picket fence around the house ran new sidewalks of wood planks, and the streets were of sandy earth. Two miles away to the east, grassy hills rolled up from level fields. Green during the cool, rainy winter and golden in the long, dry summer, the fields and hills made a pleasant playground for Julia. But soon, workers with picks and shovels would be digging foundations there, and someday Julia would design a hundred houses for those empty slopes.

The Morgan family lived comfort-

The gold rush that began in 1848 drew thousands of prospectors to the San Francisco Bay area. For many years the city retained its rough frontier character, but the region's wealth ultimately transformed it into a sophisticated urban center.

Charles Bill Morgan and his wife came west on the newly completed Transcontinental Railroad.

ably in their ample home. Eliza Morgan had an income from her father's wealth, and over the years Bill Morgan tried his hand at a variety of enterprises. He invested in stores, mines, and other businesses and served on various state commissions and as a director of the Oakland Public Schools. Later he became part owner of the Shasta Iron Works, a manufacturer of steam-powered tractors.

For their summer vacations the Morgans went to the seashore for a month or so. Usually they took the train to Santa Cruz, a hundred miles to the south. Sometimes, to escape the summer fog, they traveled all the way to Catalina Island, a then-new resort off the coast near Los Angeles. And every few years the family traveled back to

Julia grew up in this house at 14th and Brush streets in Oakland. Built on the edge of town, the Morgan home was gradually surrounded by the expanding city.

the East Coast, a six-day train ride, to visit cousins, aunts, and grandparents.

The Parmalees, Julia's grandparents, lived in Brooklyn Heights, just across the East River from Manhattan. One of Julia's cousins was married to Pierre LeBrun, a noted architect who designed, among other buildings, the Metropolitan Life Insurance Tower in New York City. Talking with LeBrun, Julia found herself intrigued by design and architecture. LeBrun noticed her appreciation of construction, and he praised her ability in mathematics and her growing talent for drawing. His encouragement and example were to have a profound effect on Julia.

Another childhood experience was also to have repercussions in her adulthood: Julia suffered an inflamed mastoid. An earache from an ordinary cold developed into a serious infection of the bones behind her ear. Trapped within the bone structure, there was no way for the infection to drain, and the pain was severe. Before the introduction of antibiotics such as penicillin, this was a serious illness. Often people would go deaf, and some even died, from mastoid infections.

Julia did not recover for quite some time, and when she had, her worried parents tried to shelter her. They wanted her to rest, stay close to home,

Julia's mother sits in the family's Oakland home. Eliza Morgan inherited money from her family, the Parmalees, thus enabling her husband to try his hand at a variety of enterprises.

Parmalee (left), Julia's elder brother, and Julia (right), four years old, pose for a portrait with their baby sister, Emma. Julia and Emma remained fast friends throughout their lives.

and live a quiet life, but they did not have much success. Although small and apparently frail, Julia was an active and energetic child, and she had an iron will. Regardless of the prevailing notions regarding the behavior of girls, she insisted on playing outside on her brothers' gym equipment. She also practiced archery, one of the few sports considered proper for young ladies at the time.

Julia's strength surprised those who knew her as a child, and after she grew up, people found it hard to believe that such a delicate-looking woman could have so much physical stamina. One of her associates, Walter Steilberg, later marveled, "The capacity of that little lady for work was just incredible." And her nephew, Morgan North, said, "She had the constitution of an ox."

Despite her refusal to obey some of her parents' rules, Julia was very close to her mother. Eliza Morgan was Julia's greatest ally. Her mother's strong belief in her helped Julia through many difficult times. The two were very much alike; both were quiet, retiring, and even shy. Like her mother, Julia was never very interested in social affairs. She was a serious girl, very attentive in school. And like many people at the time, she was fascinated by mechanical things.

Julia had the good fortune to grow up during a period of scientific advancement. The transcontinental railroad had unified the country only three years before Julia's birth, and the United States was enjoying a period of

When Julia visited San Francisco with her family, a boat ride across the bay brought them to the ferry terminus. She was to repeat the journey many times as an adult.

While visiting her mother's family in New York, Julia saw the recently completed Brooklyn Bridge. Such sights, as well as the encouragement of her cousin Pierre LeBrun, probably gave Julia her earliest inspiration to be an architect.

prosperity. In the first quarter century of her life, the volume of industrial production, the number of people employed in industry, and the number of manufacturing plants doubled. It was an exciting time. On a visit to New York, Julia had seen the famous Brooklyn Bridge under construction. The first modern skyscraper with a steel frame, the Home Insurance Company Building, was built in Chicago in 1885. Electricity had appeared, brightening houses and nighttime streets and powering the new horseless streetcars. The telephone, automobile, phonograph, typewriter, and cash register were also invented during this time. People had developed a strong faith in progress and in the improvement of human life through science and technology. The world seemed perpetually poised on the verge of new discoveries.

Just 30 years before Julia Morgan's birth, thousands of tents had covered the sand dunes of Happy Valley on San Francisco Bay, and shanties had clustered at the base of Telegraph Hill. They housed hordes of settlers drawn there by the lure of riches in gold, silver, and lumber. Many made their fortunes in California and poured their money into construction, building homes, warehouses, theaters, and every other type of structure. The gold rush transformed San Francisco into a metropolis, a great port that attracted people from all over the world.

The building boom continued unabated throughout Julia's childhood, and the future architect observed it closely. Sometimes the whole Morgan family took walks and wandered through half-built houses. Most of the new homes were big, some even larger than their own. Mrs. Morgan would point out what each of the spaces would be, and Julia would inhale the smell of the fresh wood, imagining the rhythm of the hammers and the rasp of the saws.

By the time Julia graduated from high school, San Francisco had become a busy metropolis filled with grand buildings.

On Sundays the Morgans walked east a few blocks to the First Baptist Church, a square brick structure with peaked towers at its corners. As she grew older, Julia was allowed to go further downtown. Seven or 8 blocks away, just before 14th Street crossed Broadway, stood the new city hall, a 2-story library, and the post office. By the time Julia entered high school in 1886, at the age of 14, 14th and Broadway had become the center of the city.

In high school, Julia began to think about her future. For a while she was interested in medicine. Even though most women in the medical profession were nurses, there was a growing number of female doctors, and Julia considered joining their ranks. Yet she remembered Pierre LeBrun's pride in his designs and his completed buildings, and she felt increasingly drawn to a career in architecture. She wanted to make the kinds of drawings she had seen in LeBrun's office: beautiful images of buildings and carved and molded ornaments. As she began to think about becoming an architect, Pierre LeBrun gave her all the encouragement he could. They became good friends and started writing to each other frequently.

By the time she graduated from Oakland High, Julia Morgan had decided that architecture would be her future. She knew how rare women architects were and that it would be a difficult task. But she was set on her course, she had the support of her mother, and she believed in herself. She applied and was accepted at the University of California at Berkeley.

While she prepared to enroll, Julia's resolve was strengthened by a distant event. The city of Chicago had begun plans for the World's Columbian Exposition, an elaborate world's fair to be held in 1892 to celebrate the 400th anniversary of Columbus's voyage to the New World. A Women's Building had been planned, and early in 1891 Daniel Burnham, the chief of construc-

tion, announced a competition, open only to women, for the design of the exterior of the building.

Sophia Hayden, the first woman to obtain a degree in architecture from the Massachusetts Institute of Technology, submitted the winning design. Hayden was only four years older than Julia Morgan, and her success profoundly inspired the ambitious young woman.

The Women's Building at the World's Columbian Exposition in Chicago was designed by Sophia Hayden, an MIT graduate. In a time when few women entered the architectural profession, Hayden's triumph encouraged Morgan.

The École des Beaux-Arts (pictured) was renowned as one of the world's finest schools of design, but it did not admit women to its architecture section until Morgan passed the entrance exam and won the title of éléve de l'École.

THREE

From Berkeley to Beaux-Arts

Julia Morgan entered the University of California at Berkeley in September 1890. That year, more than 450 students enrolled in its academic classes, a hundred of them women.

To get to classes Julia walked east along 14th Street to Broadway and boarded an Oakland Railroad Company streetcar. Other Oakland students, some of them classmates from high school, took the same car. At first she rode with her brother Parmalee, and after two years Emma joined them. The little streetcars, drawn by a single horse walking between the iron rails, plodded up Broadway and out Telegraph Road. Houses and shops stood scattered along the way, shaded by clusters of trees. Wooden walkways crossed the dirt street where the cars stopped.

Telegraph Road, nearly five miles long, led to the southern entrance of the campus. Students on their way to school passed through a white picket fence that marked off the university grounds and climbed an easy slope beyond Strawberry Creek. A central lawn lay between two classroom buildings and Bacon Library, and to the west a grand view stretched out across the growing town of Oakland and the wide San Francisco Bay. At the edge of the horizon the headlands of the Golden Gate were visible.

Half a dozen colleges in the East and Midwest had architecture departments, but the University of California did not. Pierre LeBrun suggested that Morgan study civil engineering instead. In her engineering classes, she would learn about the structure of buildings, as well as how to draft and how to calculate the qualities of structural elements such as beams and columns. She went to the Mining and Civil Engineering Building, a stone structure with four floors of classrooms and offices, to register. When Morgan enrolled, she met Professor Frank Soule, head of the College of Civil Engineering. A mustached man of 40 with a formal manner, he was nicknamed "the Colonel" because he had attended West Point after the Civil War.

The engineering school required that Morgan study math, science, engineering, drawing, surveying, and astronomy. It was a demanding course of study that emphasized economical solutions to practical problems. She learned mathematical formulas to predict how far a beam would span or how high a brick wall could rise. She also learned how to draw plans (views of a building's layout from above), elevations (views of a building seen straight on), and sections (views of cuts through a structure that show such features as ceiling heights and stairs). Bending over her drawing board, she learned skill with drawing pens and measuring scales. But she learned very little about architectural decoration or the essential aspect of architecture, the creation and manipulation of space.

For four years Morgan traveled back and forth from Oakland to Berkeley, not only to attend her classes but to enjoy college life. Several Greek-letter fraternities had formed on campus, and in 1890 Kappa Alpha Theta became the first sorority. Morgan pledged, and as a

When Morgan arrived in 1890 to begin her studies, the campus of the University of California at Berkeley consisted of a few buildings set into the hills.

During her college years, Morgan was a serious student, but she also joined a sorority, Kappa Alpha Theta, and formed many friendships that would last a lifetime.

Morgan spent much of her time on campus in the Mechanical Arts Building, where the civil engineering department was housed.

member she formed friendships that would last all her life. Several of her sorority sisters would later commission houses (and larger jobs) from her, and 15 years later she would build Kappa Alpha Theta's sorority house.

For Class Day, influenced by the music of the German opera composer Richard Wagner, Morgan's class of 1894 hoped to evoke the spirit of the German Middle Ages. Ben Weed, one of Morgan's classmates, had discovered a semicircular dell, later to be called

Weed Amphitheater, at the foot of the hills. The students decided to hold graduation there. They cut down a large eucalyptus tree and made an "altar" from its stump. The 97 seniors came to graduation dressed in brown monkish gowns and hoods. At that graduation, in May 1894, Julia Morgan became the first woman at the University of California to receive a Bachelor of Science degree in civil engineering. One of her classmates delivered a speech on the relationship between education and re-

Morgan's class of 1894 adapted a hollow in the campus hills, later known as Weed Amphitheater, for use during the Senior Class Day Pageant, at which Morgan played her violin.

ligion, and Morgan played the violin.

That fall the university hired an intense round-faced man of 32 to teach drawing. Bernard Maybeck, born in New York City, had spent four years in Paris, studying at the École des Beaux-Arts. He had since worked in New York and Kansas City and had arrived in San Francisco in 1889. Maybeck, an eccentric, did not fit the more conservative image generally assumed by architects. He dressed informally and sported a waist-length beard. Although he was classically trained, no style was fixed or sacred for him. One architect in the Bay Area called him "a barbarian among the strictly Renaissance men."

Bernard Maybeck, an eccentric but brilliant architect, conducted impromptu classes, which Morgan attended after her graduation from Berkeley. He encouraged her to travel to Paris and enroll at the École des Beaux-Arts.

Realizing that a number of students and graduates of the university sought instruction in architecture, Maybeck started conducting informal classes at his small newly built house, located a mile north of the campus. He offered students the chance to gain practical experience in construction as well, putting them to work building several additions to his house. When Morgan heard about Maybeck's classes, she came from Oakland to attend.

Maybeck believed that architecture should celebrate the craft of building as well as the elegance of design. Like any other art, according to Maybeck, it should create forms that evoke clear, strong feelings. Morgan later recalled his statement, "With four sticks of wood you can express any human emotion."

In addition to teaching, Maybeck also opened his own architectural practice. His first work was designing homes for university teachers. Impressed by Morgan, he hired her to help complete the drawings for a shingled, steep-roofed house planned for a lot just south of the campus. It was her first job.

Though she drew very well and knew engineering, Morgan and Maybeck realized the young architect needed more training in design. Maybeck was enthusiastic about the École des Beaux-Arts and had sent several of his protégés there. Although Beaux-Arts did not yet admit women to its architecture school, he had heard it was preparing to do so. Maybeck urged Morgan, despite the distance and the language difference, to go to Paris herself.

In Paris, Morgan discovered European architecture and culture. For relaxation between study sessions, she often strolled the streets and examined buildings.

In 1896 Julia Morgan was only 24, but she decided to go. In those years moving to Paris was a major step for a young woman. After the week-long train journey to the East Coast, she would face a 10- or 12-day voyage by ship across the Atlantic Ocean. In Paris, she would need a suitable place to live while she studied for the difficult examinations, which she would have to take in French. She knew that she might not be admitted to the École des Beaux-Arts, but the challenge of the task only increased her determination to succeed.

In the spring Morgan took the train east. She visited relatives, including Pierre LeBrun, in Boston and New York, and sailed for Europe with a female cousin as her companion. They reached Paris on June 5, 1896, and found rooms on a narrow street south of the River Seine. Morgan carried letters of introduction to a few of Maybeck's friends and looked up some acquaintances of her New York relations who helped her settle into life in Paris. She set about seeing the sights of the city, beginning with its famous cathedral. In a letter to LeBrun, she wrote, "Today we went (in the rain) to Notre Dame, and you can imagine the enjoyment—I carry Baedeker [a famous guidebook] and Nina the Dictionnaire [dictionary]." She did not mention the Eiffel Tower, built eight years before, which rose strange and modern over the old roofs of Paris.

The École des Beaux-Arts occupied several large buildings on the left bank of the Seine, where one narrow street is still called the rue des Beaux-Arts. Twice a year, several hundred men took the entrance examinations for architecture. The exams included problems in design, engineering, and the history of architecture. Forty or 50 ap-plicants, of which 15 were foreigners, might pass. A student who had gained admittance was called an *éléve de l'École*. Because the entrance exams were so difficult, many felt the title of *éléve* was prestige enough. Maybeck himself had earned nothing more.

Morgan knew she could master the exam material, but she had no assurances that the École administrators would allow her to take the exams. When her cousin left at the end of the summer, Morgan began to feel homesick. But she put her doubts and loneliness aside and determined to get to work.

Students at the École, as well as those preparing to take the entrance exams, studied in studios, or *ateliers*, with independent architects, or *patrons*, to instruct them. Maybeck had told Morgan that finding a good studio was very important because a student learned as

At the École, Morgan learned the fundamentals of classical design. Her drawings reflected the distinctive Beaux-Arts approach to architecture.

much from other students as from the teacher. He had recommended the studio of Marcel de Monclos, and Morgan joined it. De Monclos taught on the third floor of a building near the Seine, three- quarters of a mile from Morgan's rooms.

There were about 10 students in the studio. An older member collected dues that were used to pay the rent, buy coal for heat and candles for light, and pay the fee of the teaching architect. Monsieur de Monclos came by several times a week to critique student designs.

As a newcomer Morgan had to assist the senior students—who had already been admitted to the École—by adding minor details and color to their drawings. She quickly learned how to make the elegant École-style drawings. During the fall and winter, she took courses in the history of architecture and architectural design. She was learning the language, too, supplementing what she had learned in college, which was inadequate for life in Paris.

Because she was a woman, the men around her, both students and teachers, were usually polite and considerate. But for the same reason, they did not take her seriously as an architect. She was occasionally harassed by fellow students who reportedly poured water on her head and pushed her off the ends of benches. She wrote to Pierre LeBrun that one of her teachers, M. Dupulthes, ". . . has been very kind, [but] always seems astonished if I do anything showing the least intelligence, 'Ah, mais, c'est intelligent,' as though that was the last thing expected."

In February 1897, Bernard Maybeck arrived in Paris to promote a competition sponsored by the University of California for a new plan of the campus. In addition to a cash prize, the winning architect would also earn the chance to design several buildings. Philanthropist Phoebe Apperson Hearst, mother of newspaper publisher William Randolph Hearst, had financed the competition. Maybeck, the architect in charge, was visiting Europe to stir up interest.

Morgan was delighted to see someone from home. Maybeck listened to her problems and did everything he could to help, convincing the École to let her take the exam. He wrote letters to the École on her behalf and persuaded others to do the same. The school had admitted women into painting and sculpture, but not architecture classes, a situation Maybeck hoped would change.

At last, in July, Morgan was allowed to take the entrance exam, shut away by herself in a separate skylit room, very bright and very hot. She had mastered the language, but studying architecture in France still presented problems. Morgan had always designed using the U.S. system of feet and inches, and so she could not "think in meters." She made a serious mistake and did not pass.

Morgan went back to work, studying for the next exam. She wrote LeBrun that if she failed a second time she would not try again. Then, after the October exams, her patron told her that, though her work was better, the examiners had graded her especially

Morgan liked cosmopolitan Paris, but by her own admission felt homesick and alienated. Her male teachers and peers were "very kind, [but] always seem astonished if I do anything showing the least intelligence."

harshly. She had failed again. It seemed to Morgan that the school, as she wrote LeBrun, "... *ne voudrant pas encourager les jeunes filles*"—did not wish to encourage young ladies.

But the École had merely brought out her stubborn streak, and she studied harder to prepare for the next exam. That year, 1898, would be Morgan's most difficult time. She developed eye trouble, which was brought on by the strain of work and study. By summer, many of the students in de Monclos's atelier had dropped out, and she had to arrange for a new teacher.

Things began to look up, however, when she found Bernard Chaussemiche, whose optimism about Morgan's admission to the École was refreshing to the struggling student. Morgan also moved to a larger apartment, closer to the École. In October she took the exams once more, and early in November her younger brother Avery arrived to live with her and study for admission to the Beaux-Arts. Finally she learned that she had succeeded. On November 14, 1898, she wrote to LeBrun: "The Judgment was given today only, and [I] am the 13th—[behind] ten French and two foreigners—they take forty in all. It's not much but has taken quite a little effort. If it had been simply the advantages of the École, I would not have kept on after M. Chaussemiche was arranged with, but a mixture of dislike of giving up some thing attempted and the sense of its being a sort of test in [a] small way ... made it seem a thing that really had to be won."

It was about this time that Phoebe Apperson Hearst visited Paris and made a call to Morgan's rooms. Their time together helped create a bond between them. Mrs. Hearst, devoted to women's causes, was sympathetic to Morgan and her troubles, and as they were saying good-bye at the train station, Mrs. Hearst offered financial help.

But money was not the problem, as Morgan wrote in a letter thanking Mrs. Hearst for her offer. "If I honestly felt more money freedom would make my work better, I would be tempted to accept your offer—but I am sure it has not been the physical work which has been, or will be, hardest, for I am used to it and strong, but rather the months of striving against homesickness and the nervous strain of examinations. Now my brother is here, and a place is won at the Beaux-Arts, really mine now it seems, the work ought simply to be a pleasure whether housekeeping or study. Your kind words at the depot were so unexpected, so friendly, they gave and still give more help than you can guess, and I will thank you for them always."

Morgan had been in Paris for more than two years. Now the real work began.

Every month the École issued a design problem, either a simple sketch, such as a grand staircase, or a more complex project such as the design of a museum or a railway station, which required elaborate drawings. Before eight in the morning, on days when problems were assigned, Morgan left her flat for the cool streets, carrying

During the summers, Morgan traveled throughout Europe sketching architecture. She made this picture in Venice.

drawing instruments and a roll of tracing paper. Walking the four blocks to the École, she joined a crowd of other students, as nervous as she. They greeted her noisily, for they all knew who she was: the first, and for a long time the only, woman in the architecture section.

On the ground floor of the echoing old building, officials handed out the problems: They described the function of the building to be designed, the sizes of rooms and their uses, and a map of the site for which the structure should be designed. Then Morgan and the others climbed three or four floors up into large, musty attics to complete the assignment. Amid the restless clatter Morgan would find a loge, a little cubbyhole equipped with a rough drawing board. She had 12 hours to produce a design. If the problem was a sketch, she turned in her finished design to the École. If it was a complex project, she made two copies of her rough sketch, left one at the school, and from the other worked six more weeks to produce her finished drawings.

Morgan solved problem after problem and began to receive recognition for her talent. She was awarded four medals for exceptional work in design and drawing. Her achievements at school drew outside attention, which soon brought in paying work. She designed a large reception room to be built in France for a wealthy American woman.

For relief from the pressure of schoolwork, Morgan walked around Paris, looking at new buildings under construction. During the summer she traveled in Europe to view architectural sights, returning often to Italy and Germany. Her brother frequently accompanied her on these trips, during which she sketched churches and old houses.

Finally, in December 1901, after five and a half years in Paris—three of them spent at the École des Beaux-Arts—Julia Morgan became the first woman to receive the Certificat d'étude, the certificate of study, in architecture. Despite the difficulties, Morgan had prevailed, and she had received the best architectural education then available. All her life she would carry with her the prestige of her Certificat, and the skills learned at the École des Beaux-Arts.

When she boarded the ship to sail homeward early in 1902, Morgan was 30 years old.

The Mills College campanile, which Morgan designed in the Spanish mission style just after opening her private practice, was the first of many structures she would build for women's institutions.

FOUR

Building a Career

Morgan had been away from California for almost six years. When she returned, she was surprised at how time had changed her family. Her parents, now in their fifties, were older and grayer. Gardiner, her youngest brother, had grown from a teenager into an adult, and Parmalee had married and moved away. Her sister, Emma, after attending law school, had decided to marry a young lawyer named Hart North.

Outside the comfortable old house, the streets of Oakland were now lined with homes. Tall poles at the edges of sidewalks carried telephone and electrical lines. Downtown, at the city hall corner, the old gas streetlights had been replaced by electric globes, and all the streetcars were electric as well. Many well-to-do families were replacing their horse-drawn carriages with noisy automobiles. Still, Oakland seemed very small to Morgan after Paris.

Anxious to begin her career, Morgan took the ferry to San Francisco to look for work. Bernard Maybeck had only a few projects that summer, so he could not offer her a position. He sent her on to John Galen Howard, a brilliant New York architect. Howard, then 38, had attended the Massachusetts Institute of Technology and had also studied at the École des Beaux-Arts. Born in Boston, he was a tall, dignified man, charming and cultured. He had been appointed to develop the master building plan for the University of California at Berkeley.

The competition for the plan of the university had originally been won by Emile Bénard, a French architect, who in 1899 had been offered the position of supervising architect. But Bénard had also won a competition to design government buildings in Mexico City and had chosen Mexico over Berkeley. John Galen Howard was already well known in the San Francisco area. Several years before, he had supervised construction at Stanford University, south of San Francisco. The University of California offered the job of implementing Bénard's plan to Howard, whose New York firm had won fourth place in the competition. He quickly accepted.

Howard's first structure for the university was the Hearst Mining Building. For years, Phoebe Apperson Hearst had wanted a memorial for her late husband, George. Now she was anxious for it to be started. This project became Morgan's first job in Howard's office. Her talent and her long years of training

were soon obvious to Howard. But she was still alone in a traditionally male field. Soon after she began work, Howard boasted that he had "... the best and most talented designer, whom I have to pay almost nothing, as it is a woman."

After the Mining Building, Morgan worked on the drawings for the Greek Theater. At the Berkeley campus, graduation was still being held in Weed Amphitheater, the grassy bowl where Julia Morgan had played her violin. Though the site was ideal, the university felt it needed a more formal setting for graduation than tree stumps and

The Hearst Mining Building, shown here under construction, was Morgan's first job after her return from Paris. She completed the project for her employer, John Galen Howard.

wooden benches. Wealthy publisher William Randolph Hearst commissioned Howard to design permanent seats and create a theater modeled after those of ancient Greece. When construction began early in 1903, Morgan served as supervisor. Several times a week that spring, she took the ferry across the bay from San Francisco to Berkeley. She rode a streetcar up to the university and walked past the classroom buildings to the construction site. Just where the easy slope of the campus steepened into the hills beyond, the wide half-circle of seats gradually took shape among the eucalyptus trees.

Morgan soon realized that the job had fallen behind schedule. The seats would be complete for graduation ceremonies in May, but the stage backdrop would not be ready. She saved the day by hanging banners to decorate the theater and conceal the unfinished sections. On graduation day, drama students presented scenes from *The Birds*, an ancient Greek play by Aristophanes, and President Theodore Roosevelt, who had traveled all the way from Washington for the occasion, gave the commencement address. The ceremony was a great success in part because of Morgan's quick thinking.

As an architect, Morgan helped transform Weed Amphitheater at Berkeley into the Greek Theater, shown here during its dedication ceremonies.

The Greek Theater was Morgan's last job for John Galen Howard's firm. She liked the atmosphere at his office, and she thought Howard was a fine designer. She had quickly become an important member of his staff, but nevertheless faced almost constant struggle because she was a woman. Her male colleagues would not accord her the recognition she deserved. She would never be satisfied until she could work on her own.

In 1903, Morgan set up a drafting board in the carriage house of the family home in Oakland. She took the state architectural examinations and in 1904 became the first woman registered as an architect by the state of California. Her architectural practice began with a number of small houses, many for friends from college, and very soon larger commissions came her way. The first of these was from Phoebe Apperson Hearst.

A dozen years earlier, Phoebe Hearst's son, William Randolph Hearst, had enlarged a hunting lodge on the family estate at Pleasanton. His architect, A. C. Schweinfurth, had designed a large, complex house, as much like a desert fort as a country estate. Since then, Phoebe Hearst had made the Hacienda her country residence. Now she needed larger spaces for her many cultural and artistic gatherings.

Phoebe Hearst remembered Morgan very well from their meeting in Paris, and the two women had renewed their friendship at John Galen Howard's office over the drawings for the Mining Building and the Greek Theater. Hearst admired Morgan's strength and intensity and gave her the job of remodeling the Hacienda.

Morgan created several large, elaborately decorated rooms, including a music room grand enough for concerts. She filled them with tapestries, pictures, and statuary that Hearst had gathered in Europe. Morgan also extended the wide verandas of the Hacienda to create shade and protect against the hot, dry California summers. There was a covered swimming pool, too, surrounded with banks of glass doors. The design of the Hacienda foreshadowed the work Morgan would later do on the far more grandiose Hearst castle

Phoebe Apperson Hearst, who had known Morgan since her days in Paris, commissioned the young architect to refurbish her country home. Her son William Randolph Hearst would later provide Morgan with much more work.

*Morgan's redesign of Hearst's Hacienda in Pleasanton created large
entertainment spaces that the philanthropist wanted for her charitable activities.*

in San Simeon, California.

Morgan's second important commission in her first year of independent practice was a bell tower, or campanile, for Mills College, the first such tower in the West. Originally a private high school, the college stood in the fields five miles east of Oakland. In 1902 the college had received a set of eight tuned bells, and the next year it obtained a donation for a bell tower. Phoebe Hearst, an active member of the Mills community, no doubt suggested that the women's college employ a woman as its architect.

Morgan designed a five-story tower reminiscent of the California missions built by Spanish missionaries in the 18th century. El Campanil was built of plain, unadorned concrete, capped with a tile roof supported by heavy wood beams. Each bell occupied a separate arched opening. Because the tower was tall and slender, Morgan paid careful attention to the possibility of earthquakes. There had been several strong quakes in California during the last 50

years, and she knew another one would inevitably occur. She tapped her engineering knowledge to design a structure resistant to the earth's tremors.

Morgan impressed the college with her design and with her dedication and thoroughness. In the year following Morgan's work on the tower, Margaret Carnegie, wife of wealthy industrialist Andrew Carnegie, donated funds for the construction of a new library. The trustees of the college gave Morgan the commission.

In her first buildings, Morgan put into practice the principles learned during her long training at the École des Beaux-Arts. When she sat down at her drawing board, she worked first on the plan of the building's interior. She believed that the interior plan was the most important part of the design: Every room should be the proper size and relate correctly to other rooms. As she worked on a plan, Morgan sought a simple, clear arrangement of rooms: balanced and symmetrical in larger buildings, more informal in her smaller houses. She also kept in mind the character of the spaces she was creating—how high their ceilings would be, how they would be furnished, and how they would be lit by windows.

In her early work, Morgan exhibited a special talent for integrating the varied architectural traditions of the American West with the more sophisticated elements of her Beaux-Arts training. Because of her innovative approach, she would be instrumental in helping to create a new form of architecture that blended harmoniously with the California landscape.

Although as a Beaux-Arts student Morgan had followed the style of the 15th and 16th centuries and the classical models of ancient Greece and Rome, like other California architects she began to break free of these rigid constraints. California itself, relatively unbound by tradition, inspired adventure in its builders as well as its other settlers. A new generation of architects rejected norms established elsewhere as too provincial for their taste. They developed their own approach that made use of indigenous local design elements and produced dramatic spa-

Impressed with Morgan's work on the campanile, the trustees of Mills College asked her to plan a new library, pictured here. Both structures survived the 1906 earthquake.

tial effects. For example, drawing on California's highly romantic Spanish and Indian past, they incorporated the styles of the smooth, plastered Spanish missions as well as of the familiar Indian pueblos. Among the first generation of the so-called Bay Tradition innovators were Ernest Coxhead, Willis Polk, A. Page Brown, A. C. Schweinfurth, and Julia Morgan's mentor, Bernard Maybeck.

The freestyle approach adopted by Morgan and some of her contemporaries was perfect for northern California. The climate invited them to minimize the distinction between indoors and outdoors, and the spectacular views encouraged the use of large panes of glass. The abundance of native materials such as redwood helped them create the finest and most genuine form of California regional architecture ever achieved. Morgan's work, however, remained quite distinct from that of other Bay Area architects, because unlike many of them, she maintained an awareness of work being done outside California.

Morgan rapidly gained a name as an excellent architect and was swamped with commissions. With so many jobs, she could no longer work from her parents' carriage house. She moved into an office on the 13th floor of the Merchants' Exchange Building in San Francisco. Soon afterward, in the wake of the devastating earthquake of 1906, her work on the Fairmont Hotel established her reputation once and for all. Over the next decade she designed scores of churches, schools, women's clubs, and other institutional buildings. She also managed to design about 20 houses a year, and in doing so she developed a distinctive, practical layout that she used over and over again.

The downstairs of a typical Morgan house consisted of living and dining rooms on either side of an entry hall and staircase, with the kitchen and pantry placed in the rear. Upstairs, the bedrooms were sheltered by sloping eaves and often featured their own win-

Like other California architects of her time, Morgan experimented with local design elements. The state's many Spanish missions, like the one pictured here, had a particularly strong influence on Bay Area architects.

dow seats. Though she used the same basic plan over and over again, Morgan had a wonderful ability to mold her designs to the personal and budgetary needs of her clients. In fact, one woman who lived in a Morgan home for 30 years described the experience as similar to "living inside a work of art—the proportions are so classically comfortable."

Many of her homes did share one problem, however. Morgan always de-

signed kitchen counters at a height that was comfortable for her, but unfortunately, she was several inches shorter than most of her clients. According to Walter Steilberg, a longtime associate at Morgan's firm: "Someone spread the idea . . . that a woman would know more about laying out a kitchen than a man. It doesn't follow at all. As a matter of fact, that was one of her failures, I think. She always insisted on sinks being two-feet-eight [inches

The owner of this home brought Morgan a sketch by an English architect and asked her to design an interior to go with it. Morgan remarked, "Well, we have something new here. We have a front of a house and we have to put a back on!"

Morgan's design trademarks included the use of wood shingles on house exteriors and the placement of main entrances on the sides of houses. She designed this dwelling for her sister, Emma North.

high], and in every data bank you'll find the design of sinks puts them at three feet. I know many of them she put in were too low, and they had to be torn out . . . everyone [wondered] why they got backaches."

Among Morgan's reconstruction projects after the great earthquake, was the rebuilding of the interior of the First Baptist Church in Oakland. Two years later a Presbyterian congregation in Berkeley asked her to design a social hall. Because they had very little money, she created a simple redwood building with a low peaked gable. Her clients were so pleased with it that in 1910 they asked her to build a new church. St. John's Presbyterian Church has since become an architectural landmark in Berkeley. It has a taller gable than the social hall, which stands beside it. At the time, the church stood in

In St. John's Church, Morgan used structural elements such as beams and trusses to achieve a decorative effect. The building is now considered an architectural landmark.

Morgan planned St. John's Presbyterian Church to blend into the residential neighborhood surrounding it. She only placed a cross on the roof after the congregation insisted upon it.

a neighborhood of homes, so Morgan wanted it to appear, on the outside, like a large house. Only after the congregation insisted did she add a small cross to its roof.

The church had to be built on a budget of two dollars per square foot, a very low cost even then. There was no money for the decoration Morgan wanted to use, yet she was unwilling to build a plain box. She worried about the problem and finally decided that the ornamentation of the church must come from its own structural members. Morgan spent weeks over her drawing board, making small, careful sketches, but the natural appeal of the finished building belies her effort. She left the building's beautiful wood beams exposed, so the churchgoer, sitting on one of the plain pews, could see all the redwood bones of the building: the posts in the walls, the braces at the edge of the roof, even the trusses that held up the sloping roof. All were bare and completely unadorned. St. John's had an open, simple informality, like

an elegant barn. It quickly became one of Morgan's best-known buildings.

Morgan's willingness to design a church for a congregation that could not afford to pay her very much reflected one of her basic philosophies. Throughout most of her career, Morgan took every commission she was offered. She did not make money on projects such as small houses, but she charged enough on most larger jobs to break even. Morgan believed in the importance of every job she did. "Don't ever turn down a job," she told Steilberg. "The reason I tell you this is that one of the smallest jobs I ever had was a little two-room residence in Monterey. This was done when I first started in practice for myself. The lady for whom I did it was most pleased with the job, and now the lady is the chairman of the board of the YWCA. And from that has come all these fine big jobs we have."

The YWCA—the Young Women's Christian Association—would become one of Morgan's best clients.

59

For many years, much of Morgan's work came from the YWCA. In 1913 she designed the Oakland YWCA, which featured a sun-filled interior courtyard.

FIVE

Working Women

Julia Morgan lived a very different life from most women of her time. She had not married, and she never would. She took satisfaction in serving her clients and found ample reward in the creation of handsome, well-constructed buildings. She was a perfectionist who worked long, hard hours, and this complete dedication left no time for a private life of her own. She still lived at home with her parents and slept in her childhood bedroom. Much of her emotional support came from her family. Even now, with her siblings fully grown, the California Morgans remained a close-knit unit.

Morgan's sister, Emma, had married Hart North and had three children. In 1909 Morgan designed a house for them in Berkeley. Avery, the second youngest and Julia's favorite brother, had followed the older children to the University of California and then spent two years in Paris studying for the École. He had passed the entrance exams, but afterward seemed unable to find a focus for his life. He left the school and went to work. A friendly and cheerful young man, Avery had no trouble getting jobs—his trouble was keeping them. He continually repeated a pattern of working for a few months and then going out to lunch one day and never coming back.

By contrast, Gardiner, the youngest, had started a moving and storage company, as well as an insurance agency. He had also realized his dream to become a firefighter, and at 32 he had attained the position of battalion chief. But not long after, his car collided with a train and he was seriously injured. Somewhere in the family's background lurked hemophilia, a disease that keeps the blood from clotting normally: Gardiner Morgan bled to death. The family was devastated, and Julia Morgan suddenly realized that her family would not always be there to sustain her. Nevertheless, after a brief period of mourning she returned to her office.

As her business thrived, Morgan hired the few women she could find who were trained in architecture and structured her office in the atelier style she had known in Paris—a workshop arrangement that fostered interaction and learning. By 1927, 6 of her 14 office employees were women, quite a remarkable figure for the time. She gave decorative commissions to aspiring women artists, and she helped women students by contributing anonymous financial aid to university scholarship funds. Morgan thought of her staff as her family and often acted like a stern but loving mother. Dorothy Wormser, one of Morgan's associates of several years, believed that Morgan hoped to discover a commitment like her own in every new woman she hired. But each of them "... would go off and get married or something ... [and be] a disappointment," Wormser later recalled.

By 1912, at the age of 40, Julia Morgan had become a living embodiment of the ideals of the women's movement. She was an independent working woman, intelligent, well educated, and highly successful. She had already designed nearly a hundred buildings throughout the San Francisco area. It is no wonder that other women of the time followed her career with pride and used her services whenever they could.

The years during which Morgan grew up and started her career were times of increasing awareness of women's rights. As early as 1848, women had met in Seneca Falls, New York, to call for suffrage, or the right to vote. A constitutional amendment, named for suffrage movement leader Susan B. Anthony, had been defeated in the United States Senate in 1887, but a well-organized campaign for women's voting rights began in England in 1903 and was followed by a similar effort in America. In California, women won

Women in California and other western states won the right to vote in 1911, but national suffrage was not guaranteed until 1920. Morgan never considered herself a feminist, but she stood out as an example of independence and success.

the right to vote in 1911, though for the nation as a whole woman suffrage was not achieved until the ratification of the 19th Amendment in 1920.

But women also established other organizations with other goals. For example, the Women's Christian Temperance Union, founded in 1873, sought to improve the poor economic and emotional conditions in which many women lived by prohibiting the consumption of alcohol. Its members, 160,000 strong by 1890, wore white ribbons as a mark of virtue and believed that an "organized motherhood" of women could bring the gentleness and love present in their homes out into the imperfect world. Other groups, like the Charity Organization Service, were interested in bettering the morals, if not the wages, of young women. And a number of clubs, such as Sorosis, were concerned with self-improvement and

promoted the view that women should think for themselves, recognize their social responsibilities, and work to improve their community.

Another women's group, the Young Women's Christian Association, was founded in Boston in 1866. The YWCA hoped to address the problems that arose as thousands of young women streamed into the cities to look for work. These women found few adequate places to live. The YWCA created living quarters and dining rooms and offered weekly religious services, evening lectures on "virtuous" conduct, and job training for office workers. Through these and other programs, plus its practice of hiring women, the YWCA proved a significant force in the women's movement.

In 1912 Morgan began working for the YWCA, once again thanks to Phoebe Apperson Hearst. Hearst, by

The YWCA believed in a woman's right to earn a living in the workplace. The organization conducted vocational classes and employed many professional women like Morgan.

now well established in her elegant Hacienda at Pleasanton, hosted annual YWCA conferences there and had a great deal of influence in the organization. When the National YWCA purchased property for a summer conference center on the Pacific Ocean at Asilomar, California, Hearst suggested they employ Morgan as their architect.

Morgan drew up a site plan for the arrangement of buildings and roads on the grounds and designed the stone entrance gates. The following year,

among the pine-studded dunes, she created an informal stone and wood administration building that contained offices and a large central room for gatherings. She planned a series of large tents on wooden platforms to provide sleeping accommodations for 350. Within the next six years Morgan built six more structures at Asilomar. Today, the center is a California state monument.

Morgan picked up more YWCA work from Grace Merriam Fisher, one of her sorority sisters from the University of

Morgan's first project for the YWCA was the Asilomar conference center. She designed

California and the woman for whom she had designed the "little two-room residence in Monterey." Mrs. Fisher had become a director of the Oakland YWCA, and in 1913 when the chapter decided to build a new clubhouse, it needed little urging to call on Morgan. The Oakland YWCA would stand on the corner of two busy streets in the center of the bustling city. The YWCA wanted a comfortable environment for young women, but Morgan set her sights higher than that. She hoped to create a handsome and sophisticated

building, and to do so she returned to the classical models that had inspired the library at Mills College. The building's exterior would have a base of dark yellow brick, with entrances at the center of each face. A tall middle section of lighter plaster, graced with tall round-headed windows, rose above, and a fourth-floor attic made an elegant cap.

Morgan raised the main floor half a flight up from the street so that, as residents climbed the six or eight steps, the bustle of the city would fall away

the main building in 1912 and by 1918 had built six buildings at the site.

behind them. Ahead, sunlight would draw them past office space and social rooms to the center of the building, where a brightly lit atrium, ringed with classical columns and Roman arches, rose three stories to a glass roof. Like a great open heart, the court flooded the building's interior with natural light and created a serene oasis in the midst of the urban hubbub.

Around this center, Morgan provided all the facilities the YWCA usually offered: a large swimming pool in the basement, a gymnasium on the second floor, and up above, dormitory rooms for the young women. Decorative accents of ceramic tile glinted throughout the building. Morgan was so concerned that these tiles meet her standards of quality that when they were delivered

she sat down and went through thousands of them, throwing out those that did not satisfy her. Her dedication to the project paid off, for her work in Oakland and Asilomar pleased the YWCA. Over the next few years she was commissioned to design YWCA buildings in Berkeley, Palo Alto, San Jose, and San Diego.

Morgan had practiced architecture for 10 years with tremendous success. She owed her prosperity in part to her simple and productive working method. When she brought clients into her small office, she seated them in comfortable chairs around a low table. There, clients explained what they wanted in their building. If it were a home, for instance, they might describe what kind of living spaces and how

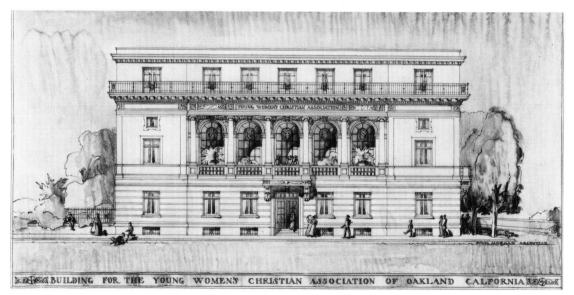

In 1913 Morgan planned the Oakland YWCA. The finished building was less ornate than the one shown in this early drawing by staffer Thaddeus Joy.

Maintaining her ties to the University of California at Berkeley, Morgan donated plans for a new Senior Women's Hall. Her design included the exposed beams typical of her work.

many bedrooms they desired. They would state how much money they could afford to spend and where the house would be built. Morgan might page through illustrated architectural books, searching for an appropriate style, and often she and her clients would visit the building site together to talk about the project. Her personal and thorough attention to planning gave many people such faith in her that they left the execution of the idea completely in Morgan's hands.

After she had a problem clear in her mind, Morgan sat at her table in the front of the drafting room and began working, carefully drawing with a T-square and triangle. She made small plans and elevations, always to an accurate scale, frequently producing half a dozen versions of an idea before everything worked to her satisfaction.

Dorothy Wormser said of Morgan's working style, ". . . she would sit and concentrate and produce those little drawings in which the whole story was foreshadowed . . . she would present that to the client, and it was always accepted, and it was the basis for the completed work."

According to Walter Steilberg, Morgan's approach to problems reflected her belief that "you couldn't monkey around with the facts of life; she felt very strongly about that. She said a lot of the bad architecture we have is because people get themselves in a jam and then they twist themselves around to get something to get out of the jam. She felt you ought to face the facts from the beginning and that's the way she was."

After she had made her drawings, a drafter would enlarge them, making sure that everything worked and adding construction notes. The final plans, from which the blueprints would be made, were drawn with India ink on thin linen.

Morgan expected this drafting work to be of the highest quality. As Walter Steilberg recalled, ". . . we had a man who was a very talented draftsman— freehand, very nice drawing. . . . She gave him a job [drawing] some sketches. She came in hurriedly and

Morgan designed the YWCA building for the Panama-Pacific International Exposition of 1915. Because its cafeteria was famous for its food, thousands of visitors flocked to the dining room, shown here.

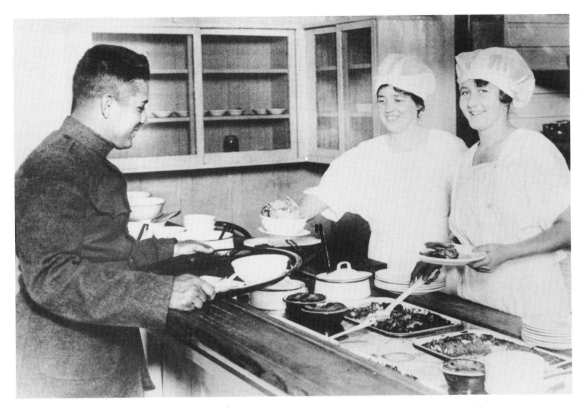

Working with the YWCA during World War I, Morgan created two comfortable, inviting "Hostess Houses" where American soldiers could relax with their friends and enjoy home-cooked meals.

took the whole thing and went to see the client that afternoon. In the course of presenting it to the clients she saw that he had drawn [an impossibly steep] stairway. . . . When she came back to the office she said, 'Well, young man, I can't deal with fiction writers.' "

"She was a perfectionist," said Wormser, "and each job was a maximum effort. Nothing was left incomplete."

Morgan's perfectionism included a rigid adherence to her own peculiar system of spelling. Architects produce written documents, known as specifications, that describe the size and quality of building materials to be used. When Morgan, who was a poor speller, wrote them, they were full of errors. Then her secretary typed them, correcting the mistakes as she went. But when Morgan rechecked the specifications, she used a red pencil to change them to reflect her original misspellings.

By 1915, with jobs under construction all over the San Francisco Bay area, Morgan could no longer rely on ferry boats and trolleys. She bought a large car but then discovered she was too preoccupied to learn to drive. She hired her brother Avery as a chauffeur and general helper, and he stayed with her for eight years.

Even as her business expanded, Morgan continued to insist on friendliness and informality in the office. She wanted everyone to be on a first-name basis, though she herself always remained "Miss Morgan." Her employees, many of whom stayed with the firm for years, were intensely loyal, and Morgan returned that loyalty. She took only enough of the firm's income to pay for the office's operating costs and her basic living expenses. What remained she generously shared with her employees—she had no interest in accumulating personal wealth. Her late

nephew, Morgan North, recalled that her personal earnings seldom exceeded $10,000 a year, and he did not think they ever reached $15,000. During the Great Depression of the 1930s, when work was scarce, she offered whatever financial help she could to her laid-off staff members until they found other jobs.

In April 1917 the United States entered World War I, which had begun in Europe in 1914. As the country mobilized, a million men were drafted into the army, and training camps were established all over the nation. The YWCA set up "Hostess Houses" at the camps, where soldiers could visit with their families and friends. Doing her part for the war effort, Morgan designed two Hostess Houses for California

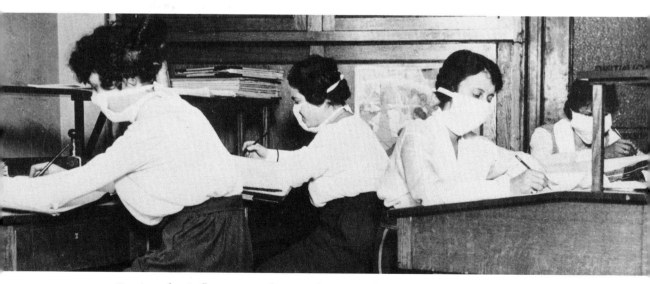

During the influenza epidemic of 1918, which exacted a higher death toll than had World War I, Morgan lost her dear friend Phoebe Apperson Hearst. This photograph shows office workers wearing masks to protect themselves against the virus.

camps, using light colors and homey touches to make them as unmilitary as possible.

In late 1918, after World War I had ended, Morgan received an offer from the National YWCA to become its staff architect. It was a tempting opportunity, but it required a move to the Midwest. She felt unable to go. As she wrote to Phoebe Apperson Hearst, "They have asked me to come to them permanently and over look their building plans nationally—but on [account] of my family here it would not be possible to accept, attractive as it could be in the way of service . . . " By "family" she meant both relatives and office staff; she did not want to leave either.

In that same letter, written in March 1919, she tried to thank Hearst for all her years of help. ". . . through [all my life] is the thread of your kindness since those Paris days when you were so beautifully kind to a most painfully shy and homesick girl. My mother's and yours are the greatest 'faith' put in me, and I hope you both know how I love and thank you for it."

Since the end of the war, a virulent strain of influenza had swept across the world, killing millions. When Morgan wrote her letter, Hearst had already fallen ill. She did not recover, and died on April 13, 1919, at the age of 76. It had been 20 years since the women had first met in Paris, and Morgan had lost a close and influential friend. Although upset and disheartened, Morgan could not mourn for long.

William Randolph Hearst had come west from New York to be with his

Morgan poses for a snapshot with Emma North's children. Over the years, Morgan drew closer to the North family, having never married or had children of her own.

ailing mother. Upon her death, he took control of the enormous Hearst fortune and the family's extensive properties, including the huge ranch at San Simeon. It was natural for him to come to his mother's architect when he decided to build. Morgan was not surprised at all when he walked into her office on an April morning in 1919, but she could never have guessed that Hearst would keep her busy for most of the rest of her career.

William Randolph Hearst commissioned Julia Morgan to build his mansion at San Simeon. She worked for him for 18 years.

S I X

The Hearst Castle

On a bright summer morning several years after William Randolph Hearst's first visit to her office, Julia Morgan stood on the summit of Camp Hill in the Santa Lucia Mountains. She stared west, down the sloping California hills to the village of San Simeon and beyond to the Pacific Ocean, five miles away and nearly a quarter of a mile below.

Around her rang the noise of construction: the rhythmic banging of hammers, the calls of workers, the grinding of a concrete mixer. She stood before a large churchlike house, its rough concrete walls unfinished. High above, carpenters assembled wooden forms for the pouring of the second- and third-floor walls and for a pair of ornate towers that would loom over the hilltop. People already called the place Hearst's Castle.

Before her lay a brick terrace, a scattering of native oaks, and the roofs of three large guesthouses situated just down the slope. The center house, called only House C, was not yet complete, though its concrete walls had been poured and its roof tiles laid. A large hole gaped in the roof and the dust of smashed concrete drifted above it. Morgan came down to the building site from San Francisco by train several times a month, and that July morning she had found the bricks and concrete of House C's chimney half-demolished and the workers grumbling as they jackhammered the rest.

A week earlier Hearst had come west from New York with his family for their summer vacation at San Simeon. In past years they had camped on the hill in large army tents, but now that two guesthouses were complete, they moved into the larger one, House A— Casa del Mar, or the House of the Sea. Hearst, however, did not like the look of House C. Walter Steilberg remembered the episode in an interview years later: "The fireplace had been located on the long side of one of the living rooms. He came in, and I was there when he said, 'No, I don't like it there. Take it out and move it over here.' And it was all built! Chimney going clear up to the roof, and everything, and the foundation . . . down the hillside." Morgan protested to Hearst strongly. She had a monthly budget for her work, and she knew the change would be expensive and time consuming. Though she and Hearst had gone over her plans carefully and had talked about the house many times, he had

Construction of the various buildings on Camp Hill proceeded simultaneously. In this photograph, House C is shown at the left and House A to the right, with Hearst's temporary quarters in the foreground.

never complained about the location of the fireplace.

But Hearst was used to having things his way. The only child of a miner who struck it rich in the gold rush, Hearst had been given control of the *San Francisco Examiner*—owned by his father— when he was only 24. He had gone on to amass a fortune in publishing, and as he neared 60 he presided over an empire that included 6 magazines and 13 newspapers. Now, glaring down at Morgan on Camp Hill, Hearst told her that he

When it was finally finished, after being moved twice, the fireplace in House C made a rich complement to the cottage's decor.

was used to changing the layout of his newspapers whenever he pleased and that at San Simeon he should surely be free to move a chimney once in a while. Morgan made the change.

In an era of wealthy men, Hearst was one of the richest and most influential. When he was only 33 he had moved to New York and purchased the *New York Morning Journal*. His strident editorials against Spanish rule in Cuba had helped bring on the Spanish-American War in 1898. He had also been elected to Congress twice, but he had never been accepted into high society. In a way, his decision to build an extravagant castle at San Simeon was his response to the Astors and the Vanderbilts: They had built their own mansions, and so would he. But whereas their architects favored English and French models, both he and Morgan agreed that San Simeon should be Spanish. He already owned a collection of Spanish and Italian architectural pieces; now he could buy even more. As his mother once said, "Every time Willie feels badly, he goes out and buys something."

From the very beginning, Hearst had made it clear that he wanted Morgan to execute his own ideas about San Simeon. Walter Steilberg later recalled what happened when Hearst first arrived at Morgan's office on that April morning in 1919 with a book under his arm:

"Miss Morgan," he said, "I would like to build something up on the hill at San Simeon. I get tired of going up there and camping in tents. I'm getting a little old for that. I'd like to get something that would be more comfortable. The other day I was in Los Angeles, prowling around second-hand book stores as I often do, and I came upon this stack of books called Bungalow Books. Among them I saw this one which has a picture—this isn't what I want, but it gives you an idea of my thoughts about the thing, keeping it simple—sort of a Jappo-Swisso bungalow."

They laughed together at Hearst's notion of a "Jappo-Swisso bungalow," meant to refer to an informal house with a gently sloping roof and wide, sheltering eaves. The castle, however, would be very different from that. As they talked, Morgan realized that Hearst—with his huge collection of art stored in warehouses on both coasts— needed a building at San Simeon that would serve both as a house and as a museum.

After he left her office that day, she bent over her drafting table and began a series of drawings for the west elevation of the main house, an image of the house's front seen straight on. Hearst returned to her office every several days, and before long they had settled on their basic idea: a tall, decorated main building with two towers, and three smaller houses for guests situated below it on the hillside. Morgan worked on plans for the big house for weeks, worrying especially over the design of the towers. Their tops changed from simple tile roofs to domes, then to old mission bell towers. She eventually settled on ornamented towers similar to those of country churches in Spain.

Morgan planned a castle that looked

Before he decided to build on his 270,000-acre estate, Hearst camped with his family and friends on the hilly property above the Pacific Ocean. Camp Hill is shown here before construction began.

Morgan planned a main house and three guest houses for San Simeon. The Casa Grande clearly shows the combined influence of Morgan's classical European training and her interest in local Spanish mission architecture.

something like an old Spanish mission, with smooth walls that would reflect the dry California sunlight; intricate decorations that cast deep shadows over the doorways; and plain tile roofs. Eventually Hearst's Castle would become America's most flamboyant and ostentatious architectural gesture, a 144-room celebrity playground where Hollywood stars such as Greta Garbo and Charlie Chaplin would gather to relax. And it would gain mythical status as the mansion, Xanadu, featured in Orson Welles's cinema classic, *Citizen Kane.*

While Morgan prepared the plans, she had to decide how to build what she was drawing. Hearst's ranch at San Simeon, started when his father bought land there in 1865, had grown to 270,000 acres—420 square miles of oak-studded mountains and grass-filled valleys. Building there would be a chal-

lenge. The ranch lay on an isolated stretch of the California coast, halfway between San Francisco and Los Angeles. All building materials would have to be brought in by truck or ship, which posed difficulties because the serpentine dirt road to the top of the mountain was often flooded by rainstorms. The nearest town with a railroad station was San Luis Obispo, 40 miles to the south, and it could only be reached by unpaved roads atop the ocean-side cliffs.

To solve the problem, Hearst rebuilt an old whaling pier at San Simeon village. The job was also made easier by the choice of concrete—which would make the houses fireproof and earthquake-sound—as the building material. Unlike the heavy, awkward steel beams that would otherwise be required, concrete walls could be built from cement (which came in bags), sand, gravel, and bundles of steel reinforcing bars. Cement and steel bars could be unloaded easily from small freighters at the wharf and trucked up the long hill. Sand was readily available at the site, and the bedrock of Camp Hill made excellent gravel.

Finally work began on the hilltop. Morgan had hired many of the construction crew herself, especially the artisans who crafted the decorations and finishing work. She first had to break down the workers' resistance to living in tents on an isolated mountainside, but she eventually managed to recruit the 60 or 70 crew members she needed for the project: carpenters, tile setters, concrete handlers, gardeners, and the like. She sent architects from her office to oversee the work and visited as often as she could.

Morgan preferred to spend most of her time in Oakland and San Francisco,

both to oversee her office and to be close to her mother, who had recently suffered a paralyzing stroke. She was also concerned about her father, who had been badly affected by his wife's illness. It seemed to her that even his mustache drooped with sadness. She still lived at home, but the added pressure of her duties at San Simeon made her impatient with the time she spent on the ferries every day. Thus in 1920 she purchased a pair of old houses on Divisadero Street, near the crest of a San Francisco hill. She renovated them, turning them into a single building divided into several apartments. Keeping one apartment for herself, she rented out the rest of them to young women. From this location she could walk down a few blocks to California Street and take cable cars directly to the Merchants' Exchange Building.

Though she had no time to visit her

Hearst had this old whaling pier refurbished to handle shipments of building supplies to San Simeon.

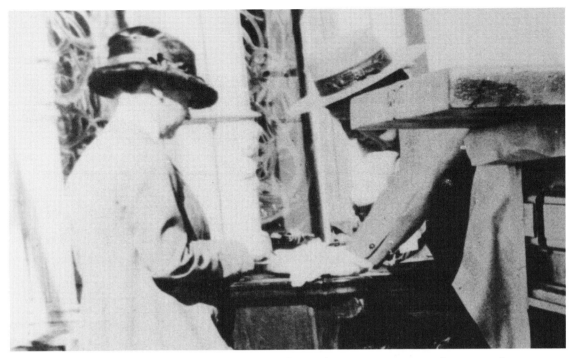

Morgan draws while Hearst watches. The imaginative architect and the fickle millionaire established a successful working relationship.

mother during the day, at night after work she often went with her brother Avery to the Ferry Building and took a boat across the bay. They drove from the Oakland dock through quiet residential streets to their parents' house. Upstairs, she talked quietly with her mother, giving her the news of the office and sometimes by a dim light reading one of Eliza's favorite stories. Occasionally Morgan stayed with her all night, napping in her chair while her mother slept. As dawn crept through the windows, Morgan would kiss her mother good-bye and go downstairs to have breakfast with her father and brother. By eight o'clock she would be back at work again.

Years before, as a young student in Paris, Morgan had developed a work

routine that came in handy during the years she spent building San Simeon: 10 or 12 hours of work each day, 6 days a week, with 5 or 6 hours' sleep at night. The only way to get to San Simeon was by taking a six-hour train ride, but she did not let that disrupt her work schedule. When it was time to visit the work site, she boarded an evening train in San Francisco for an overnight ride. The train had Pullman sleeper cars, and most of the passengers crawled into a berth and slept until they arrived in Los Angeles the next morning. But Morgan always took an upper berth, which allowed her to prop herself up with her drawing board and work until the train reached San Luis Obispo at about 2:00 A.M. From there, a taxi drove her to San Simeon—

a trip that on the miles of dirt road might take three hours in fog or storm. At the Castle she rested for a couple of hours and then met Hearst for breakfast.

Often it seemed as if the San Simeon project were one long struggle to satisfy a fickle client and circumvent his interference, for Hearst constantly changed his mind about what he wanted. When Morgan designed the Casa Grande (the large house, or main house), for instance, she had to solve the extremely difficult problem of how to incorporate the many decorated ceilings from Spanish castles, choir stalls from European churches, intricate Italian windows, French paintings, and sculptures from around the world that Hearst owned. Her client had collected so much art that he had lost track of what he owned. Staff from Morgan's

Architects, laborers, and Hearst himself lived in tents on the isolated hillside while the buildings of San Simeon were under construction.

This view of The Casa Grande in progress shows the towers being rebuilt to accommodate carillon bells. Construction materials are piled on the slope below.

office were constantly measuring and photographing the warehoused collection.

Morgan had drawn the plan of the Casa Grande in the shape of a capital *I*. A small lobby led into an immense assembly room, 80 feet from side to side, that made up the bottom line of the *I*. While under construction, the huge concrete room was dark, bare, and damp, cluttered with building materials, and noisy due to work on the library overhead. Yet when Morgan visited she could already envision the finished space, its intricately carved Spanish ceiling lit by clusters of electric lights, the long tapestries hung on the walls, and old choir seats lining its long walls.

Halfway down the length of the room stood a huge, ornate fireplace. Small doors on either side of it opened onto the dining room, or refectory, which was 60 feet long and formed the upright of the *I*. Shafts of sunlight poured into the high space through pointed Gothic windows, and a table long enough to seat 40 people would run down the center of the room. Flags from the Italian city of Siena were to hang from the carved ceiling.

At the far end of the refectory, beyond a decorated arch, a smaller dining room made the top of the *I*. It, too, would have an ornate ceiling, antique European furniture, and tapestries. Through a small alcove lay an exit. From front to rear the building was nearly 150 feet long, and to Morgan's plans Hearst wanted to add yet another large wing with kitchens and servants' rooms.

Morgan had labored to create a design that would meet Hearst's needs, but to

After Morgan had designed a symmetrical I-shaped layout for the main building, Hearst decided to add a wing (pictured here under construction) to house a kitchen and servants' quarters.

no avail: On her plans for the Casa Grande he scrawled a note to lengthen the assembly room. He had always felt free to write directly on her careful drawings, and now it seemed that he wanted to change not just a detail but the building itself. Morgan would have to redraw the plans completely. She knew that Hearst, because of his wealth, lived in an unreal world in which he expected things to be exactly as he wanted them. Thus, Morgan could not argue with him, and she altered the layout. Because she was so willing to adapt to her client's desires, Hearst and she worked together very well . . . most of the time.

As work continued at San Simeon, which Hearst had begun to call the Cuesta Encantada, or the Enchanted Hill, progress was often made in spite of Hearst's meddling. The story of the swimming pools typifies the pattern. Morgan began the first pool, down the slope to the northeast of the guesthouses, in 1922. It was a big, ordinary swimming pool that Hearst did not like. Within three years Morgan enlarged and rebuilt it, but Hearst was still not satisfied. In 1928, she began to rebuild the pool, now more than a hundred feet long, a third time, creating a grand stairway that stepped down from the guest houses toward its expanse of blue water. A marble deck surrounded the pool, while at each end curved rows of antique Roman columns provided shade. Under the porticoes, bathers could admire Hearst's collection of marble statuary.

Hearst had bought the facade of an ancient temple, which he wanted incorporated into a bathhouse with changing rooms. Morgan convinced him to use the structure as decoration instead and set a statue of Neptune, the Roman god of the sea, into the facade's triangular gable. The place became known as the Neptune Pool, and at last Hearst was pleased.

Even before the outdoor pool was finished, Hearst wanted to build facilities for swimming indoors. Morgan designed a large, plain building northeast of the main house, placed tennis courts on the roof, and lined the floor around the pool with venetian-glass tiles. The Roman Pool, a glittering blue grotto that took 3 years to build, cost $400,000. Yet the outdoor Neptune Pool was far more attractive, and few guests ever used the indoor addition.

In the midst of Morgan's hectic years at San Simeon, her father suffered a massive stroke. Although Morgan's mother remained alert and clearheaded, she was weak and unable to care for her husband, who lay in his bed dazed, paralyzed, and unresponsive. When the old man fell ill, Avery Morgan quit his job as his sister's driver and assumed the full-time task of nursing his father. He threw himself into the work, filled with hope at every sign of improvement and devastated by each new symptom of decline. Bill Morgan lived for almost a year, but there was nothing his son could do to save him. When his father finally died in 1924, Avery suffered a nervous breakdown.

Despite these difficulties, Morgan stayed on the job at San Simeon. She had no way of knowing it would take her 18 years to complete or that she would draft a mountain of architectural drawings (preserved to this day in the San Simeon archives) for this project alone. Of all the achievements of her brilliant career, Morgan would be best remembered for Hearst's Castle at San Simeon. Her triumph, however, would have a high price, both financially and emotionally. Six months after he moved the fireplace in House C, Hearst pointed to the chimney and said, "No, that was a mistake. Take it out and put it back where it was." The whole thing was ripped out once more and rebuilt in its original place.

Though they differed, Morgan and Hearst developed a strong relationship. He admired her work and depended on her management abilities. She agreed with his desire for quality and was

Hearst asked Morgan to make numerous changes to the outdoor pool before he was satisfied with it.

84

impressed at how easily he could understand architectural drawings. Whenever Hearst was at San Simeon, Morgan was always willing, if summoned by telegram, to take the next train from San Francisco to San Luis Obispo. She would, in fact, make the journey a total of more than 500 times. Between 1919 and 1942, Morgan devoted the greater part of her energy to the San Simeon project. And in return, in a world where men often considered women their intellectual inferiors, WilliamRandolph Hearst worked with Julia Morgan as an equal. Of their unique relationship, Morgan's associate Walter Steilberg later said, "Miss Morgan and Mr. Hearst had this in common—they were both long-distance dreamers. That didn't mean that they necessarily had the same dreams, but they were looking way, way ahead."

The original pool is shown at the left and the final version—the Neptune Pool—is pictured above.

The Berkeley Women's City Club had a distinct Gothic flavor. It featured an indoor swimming pool and various courtyards, and its members ate off china designed by Morgan to complement the tile used throughout the building.

SEVEN

Landmark Years

San Simeon dominated Morgan's life for years, but it was by no means her only work. She continued designing buildings for the YWCA in such places as Fresno, Pasadena, and Long Beach, California, and in Salt Lake City, Utah. She built YWCAs for Chinese and Japanese women in San Francisco. For Methodists and Presbyterians she created residence "missions" in San Francisco that served as schools and as social clubs. Morgan also designed structures for local groups, such as the Sausalito Women's Club, and buildings such as the Claremont Club in Berkeley and the Foothill Club in Saratoga. One of her most attractive buildings of the period was the Studio Club in Hollywood.

During this period Morgan also collaborated with Bernard Maybeck on the Phoebe Apperson Hearst Gymnasium at the University of California at Berkeley. Commissioned by William Randolph Hearst as a memorial to his mother, the gym featured exercise rooms surrounding a swimming pool on three sides and a plain concrete exterior that was decorated with molding, columns, and arched windows. Ornate urns stood at entrances and around the pool.

Morgan also did some work for Hearst's companion Marion Davies, a comic-film actress. Hearst had been married to his wife Millicent for almost 20 years, and the marriage had produced five sons. But by the early 1920s the Hearsts' relationship was in trouble. Several years before, Hearst had met Marion Davies, 35 years his junior, and now he no longer bothered to conceal his infatuation with her. His wife refused to give him a divorce, and the Hearsts separated.

Tired of her cramped dressing room at MGM studios, in 1926 Davies decided to build a 14-room bungalow on the MGM lot. She convinced Hearst to help pay for it, and he hired his architect, Julia Morgan, for the job. Later, in 1930, Morgan served as architect for a children's clinic financed by Davies in Los Angeles.

By the mid-1920s, Morgan had buildings under construction all over California. Because she made it her policy to visit each one as it was being built, she soon discovered that she spent most of her time traveling. She decided to begin flying and chartered a Lockheed Vega to take her to the jobs. At the same time, she expanded her staff

and moved her firm into larger offices on the 11th floor of the Merchants' Exchange Building. She also hired an office manager to handle the tasks for which she no longer had time.

During this period Morgan accepted a commission for one of the few buildings she would design outside California: the Honolulu, Hawaii, YWCA. When work began on this YWCA, she had to forego her usual on-site inspections, for Hawaii was too far away to visit regularly. No aircraft yet flew to

At Hearst's request, Morgan designed this bungalow for Marion Davies on the grounds of MGM Studios.

the islands, and ships took several days each way. Instead she sent staffers—first Bjarne Dahl, and later Ed Hussey—as her representatives in Honolulu. But when the YWCA opened in 1927, Julia Morgan took a cruise ship to the islands to attend the festivities herself. She was quite proud of the structure, which remains an architectural landmark today.

The demands of Morgan's hectic schedule were intensified by a decline in her mother's health. Over the years

Eliza Morgan had grown steadily weaker, but whenever either of her daughters spoke to her of moving out of the big, old Morgan house, she would not hear of it. She argued that she was used to the house, saying that she was too old to change and would be lost in another place.

By the late 1920s, however, the sisters decided their mother must move, whether she wanted to or not. There was room enough on Emma North's property for a small house, so Morgan

The Phoebe Apperson Hearst Gymnasium for Women on the Berkeley campus of the University of California set swimming pools and exercise rooms in surroundings reminiscent of ancient Greece and Rome.

designed a cottage. Its largest room, upstairs, was an exact copy of their mother's bedroom in Oakland.

On Thanksgiving Day of 1928, Emma's son Morgan drove down to Oakland. He brought his grandmother back to the North house for the holiday meal. After dinner, instead of taking Eliza Morgan back to Oakland, her family carried her through the yard and upstairs into her new room. Eliza Morgan lay back in her bed and went peacefully to sleep. She never mentioned the change, and the family was never sure she noticed it. She lived happily in the little house until her death a year later.

The Eliza Morgan cottage may have been Julia Morgan's smallest building in Berkeley, but that year she also began work on one of her largest struc-

When the Honolulu YWCA opened in 1927, Morgan made a trip to Hawaii to attend the dedication ceremonies. She was 55 at the time.

tures there. The Berkeley Women's City Club was to stand a block south of the university campus. In its design, Morgan combined Gothic and Romanesque styles to create a handsome six-story club and hotel. She used unadorned concrete for its soaring vaulted ceilings, displaying once again her talent for using structural materials as design elements. The club, in many respects reminiscent of San Simeon, enjoys landmark status today.

In both volume and quality, Morgan's achievements had been extraordinary. In 1929 the University of California bestowed special recognition on the woman who had been the school's first female civil engineering graduate 35 years earlier, awarding her an honorary Doctor of Laws degree. Overcoming her dislike of publicity, Morgan sat for an official portrait, the first made of her since childhood, and, although nervous, she attended the commencement celebration that May. She found, to her surprise, that she enjoyed herself.

At the age of 57, Morgan had accomplished more than most people do in a lifetime, but she had no intention of slowing down. She started a major project with Bernard Maybeck—the design and construction of a new campus for Principia College in St. Louis, Missouri. One of the first buildings designed was the chapel, in the style of a New England church, with a tall white steeple. The classroom buildings and dormitories were English Gothic structures similar to the colleges at Oxford University in England, built of brick with narrow windows and steep roofs.

The college wanted the first buildings finished in 1931. Maybeck set up an office in St. Louis, staffed with people from San Francisco. The rush to build created severe problems, and soon Maybeck felt unable to control the job. In 1932 Morgan became the architect in charge of construction, and Maybeck stayed on as a design consultant.

That year Morgan also designed one of her last women's clubs, the new YWCA Residence Club in San Francisco. The site was on Powell Street, where the cable cars that ran by the front door would give the club's working residents easy transportation downtown. As she did with so many of her buildings, Morgan designed ample social rooms and a lush garden visible from the dining room. She met with the building committee every week in the YWCA building to discuss the plans. The board consisted of several prominent, wealthy women of San Francisco who were accustomed to having their way.

Morgan was always mild and polite to her clients, but she had 10 years of experience dealing with such difficult customers as William Randolph Hearst. According to Hettie Marcus, one of the YWCA board members, Morgan "didn't ever fight for anything. She would just say something in a quiet way . . . just quietly did what she wanted to do."

As Mrs. Marcus noted, Morgan also kept in mind the human needs of the people who would use her buildings. "One time when we met with her, things were going along, and she said, 'I found that we have a little extra space here,' and she said, 'My idea is to have one or two little private dining rooms with little kitchenettes so that the girls can invite their friends, and cook a little meal and have a little private dining room.' Well, a lot of the Board opposed it. They said, 'These are minimum wage girls there. Why spoil them?' And she said, 'That's just the reason. That's just the reason.' I remember things like that. The next time that we were together she [had] planned these rooms."

Meanwhile, San Simeon continued to occupy most of Morgan's time— Hearst was still building. Somewhere in Europe Hearst had found a collection of tuned bells that he now wanted fitted into the high towers of the Casa Grande. Morgan struggled to come up with the right plan for remodeling the towers, then she made a set of sketches and took the train to San Luis Obispo.

When she reached the Castle, she and Hearst walked through the Assembly Room and out the western door. The front courtyard now had its fountain, and the high west front of the

Hettie Marcus recalled that, when designing the YWCA Residence Club in San Francisco, Morgan "just quietly did what she wanted to do," despite the board's opposition to some of her plans.

Julia Morgan meets a baby elephant at San Simeon. Hearst kept a menagerie of exotic animals on the grounds. A 1931 Fortune *magazine article reported that on the estate "wild beasts will howl of a moonlit night."*

building was nearly complete. Morgan looked up at the twin towers. They rose up as square masses, past the gabled roof over Hearst's third-floor sitting room. Above that they became eight-sided, with open arches. Each had a tall, slender top with a plain octagonal cap, recalling the Spanish mission style on which they were based.

Morgan explained her sketches to Hearst. She proposed adding another level to the tops of the towers because Hearst wanted to build a fourth floor between them for what he called the Celestial Suite. The lower sections of the towers would become bedrooms, and above that level the towers would be strengthened to carry water tanks. A smaller structure with narrow arches would be added to carry the bells.

Hearst was delighted, especially with the tile work and decorative sculpture

Morgan had added—he had always thought the towers were too plain. He planned to purchase a pair of gilded Venetian weathervanes for the tops. The construction foreman, who had come out to listen to their talk, peered at the sketches and up at the towers and said it amazed him how Morgan could create such beautiful structures. Even the modest architect felt a tinge of pride at her solution to the bell tower problem. Once again she had met the challenge of Hearst's ever-changing demands.

The Casa Grande was indeed an imposing sight—and an appropriate base for Hearst's operations—when it was finally completed.

93

Hearst asked Morgan to build on other parts of his estate as well. He grazed cattle on his 270,000 acres and employed a large ranch staff, who lived in San Simeon. Around 1930 Hearst decided to set up another headquarters in the northeast corner of his property. He hired Morgan to design the mission-style complex of Los Milpitas, near Jolon and the old Spanish mission of San Antonio de Padua. The new complex looked much like the nearby mission itself—some visitors felt Morgan's work was more handsome than the original.

Then, at the Cuesta Encantada, Hearst asked for a great luxury. Except for swimming, his main form of exercise was horseback riding. The summer sun was often intense, and Hearst wanted to be able to take horseback rides in the shade. Morgan told him that this would require the construction of a very long roof over a riding

The Refectory in The Casa Grande, which served as the dining room, epitomized Hearst's love of the ornate. The room housed items collected during his many trips to Europe.

Celebrities from all walks of life gathered at San Simeon, but Hearst (to left of candlestick) insisted that condiment bottles remain on the elegant dining room table for meals.

This bedroom was but one of dozens in The Casa Grande. Though every room in the house was jammed with decorative artifacts, many more objets d'art were stored in warehouses until they were auctioned off during the depression.

trail. They settled on an arrangement of concrete columns that would support overhead latticework covered with vines. The pergola was built to accommodate a tall person riding a tall horse and wearing a tall hat. It made a loop more than a mile long.

To his employees, his friends, and even his sons, Hearst was "the Chief." As he settled into the Casa Grande it became, in equal parts, the headquarters for his publishing empire, a personal museum, and a private resort for dozens of guests from the glittering world of Hollywood. Despite the millions of dollars he spent on San Simeon and the ornate richness of its furnishings and decor, to Hearst it was always "the ranch." From it, he ruled his kingdom.

Author Ludwig Bemelmans, who once spent a weekend at San Simeon, later described the Refectory. His words capture the peculiar combination of imported glamour and folksy comfort that characterized "the ranch":

I walked through the dining hall. It is

formidable Gothic. Up above hang the old, torn battle flags of the city of Siena. Below is a table the length of the room, so big that whoever sits at the far end is very small. Here again is a fireplace that devours the trunks of trees. The flames, behind a glass screen, leap up to the height of a man. At the right is an armorer's anvil, arresting and beautiful, but the base of it is fixed to hold nuts, and on top of the anvil lies a hammer to crack the nuts. There are tall silver candlesticks all along the center of the long refectory table, and between them stand, in a straight line and in repeating pattern, bottles of catsup, chili sauce, pickled peaches, A-1 sauce, salt and pepper in shakers that are cute little five-and-ten-cent figures of Donald Duck with silvered porcelain feet, and glasses in which are stuck a handful of paper napkins.

On August 24, 1932, when Morgan was 60, Jim LeFeaver, Morgan's office manager, sent a telegram to William Randolph Hearst. Miss Morgan, it said, would be incapacitated for a short time. At first her condition seemed to be a bad cold, but it was not. Her illness would change her life.

Morgan's years of work on San Simeon yielded a sprawling complex of buildings tucked away in the California hills.

Morgan, reserved and modest, never sought fame. Instead, she hoped to remain anonymous, much like the medieval designers of cathedrals, and allow her work to speak for itself.

EIGHT

Peace to the Mind

Morgan's left ear, which had troubled her since childhood, had become infected once again. As had happened in her youth, the mastoid spaces in the bone behind her ear filled with the infection. There were still no antibiotics available to treat a serious infection such as this. The best treatment was to open the bone, relieve the painful pressure, and allow the infection to drain.

Morgan's recovery from surgery took longer than expected. On September 21, 1932, Hearst sent her a telegram with his own advice. "Dear Miss Morgan, I think if you took a bottle of English or rather Irish stout every day it would do you a lot of good. You eat so little the porter [beer] would give you strength. May I send you some Dublin stout? Sincerely, W.R. Hearst." On October 1 Morgan wrote to him that she had gotten back to work on the hill the preceding Thursday. Two weeks later Hearst replied that he was "... glad to see you have lots more strength and energy after the operation."

But the infection flared up again, and Morgan had to return to the hospital. This time the surgeon removed her entire inner ear. In December she wrote Hearst: "What happened to me was that not healing, the innermost ear chamber became re-infected and the miserable sequence of operations all had to be gone through with again. It looks now as though the healing would be perfect, and I'll be as good as ever soon."

Characteristically, Morgan did not tell Hearst the bad news. During the operation, the surgeon had accidentally cut one of her facial nerves. The left side of her face was paralyzed and began to droop, as if she had had a stroke. The physician, horror-stricken by his mistake, never charged her a fee. Morgan understood how bad he felt, and, knowing that his wife loved orchids, sent her some every subsequent year at Christmas. (It was an especially forgiving gesture; Morgan despised orchids.)

Not only did the operation disfigure

her, but the removal of her inner ear upset her balance. She had dizzy spells and could walk a straight line only with difficulty. One of her employees later remarked that Morgan still kept her sense of humor. "Her inner ear was damaged, her sense of equilibrium, and she would talk about walking down the street and trying to pass a [staggering] drunk."

Hearst wrote to her, asking that she take it easy. "Do not worry. Occupy yourself with anything that keeps you quiet,—jigsaw puzzles or something of that kind . . . there is no architecting on the Hill."

Morgan's physical troubles seemed to echo the problems of America's economy, which had also lost its balance in recent years. After the stock market crash of 1929, the country had slipped into the Great Depression. By 1933, even Hearst's enormous wealth was affected, and he telegraphed Morgan in March to restrict operations at the Enchanted Hill to necessary work only.

Nonetheless, Hearst continued to provide Morgan with plenty of work. In northern California, near Mt. Shasta, he owned 65,000 acres that stretched for miles along the McCloud River near the town of Wyntoon. Years before, Bernard Maybeck had built a remarkable forest castle for Phoebe Apperson Hearst on the site. In the 1920s, Morgan had remodeled the superintendent's house and designed tennis courts and a swimming pool there. But the grand, rugged castle at Wyntoon had burned. Instead of replacing it, Hearst

wanted to build a collection of smaller houses. He invited Morgan up to Wyntoon, where she stayed for nearly a month. In the cool mountain air she fished the river and walked the miles of trails that crisscrossed the property.

Of course, Morgan did more than rest. She sadly set about having the great ruin of Maybeck's castle demolished, and she spent hours walking along the riverbanks with Hearst, dis-

After her illness and operation, Morgan relaxed on the grounds of Wyntoon and fished in the McCloud River. This photograph reveals the effect that the botched operation had on her appearance.

cussing where the new houses should stand. Among the tall pines that reminded them of Germany's Black Forest, they decided to build in the Bavarian style.

As she set about planning Wyntoon, Morgan began to feel the effects of her age. All her life she had drawn on a seemingly inexhaustible fund of energy, often surviving for days on nothing more than Life Savers and black coffee. Now she was irritated to discover that her energy had begun to run out. She considered taking a vacation, or at least making a change of scene, and bought a small cottage among the pines in Monterey. At first she put her drawing board at one end of the living room. Later she remodeled the interior, building a large studio on the second floor where she had ample room to design. She began to take the train down to Monterey on weekends, but she did not intend to stop working.

Hearst, knowing that Morgan loved to travel, sent her to Europe. She was to relax and do architectural research for Wyntoon. He laid out a route that would take her from Italy to Germany and through England and Wales.

She would travel by private car. "The automobile is going to be my automobile," Hearst wrote her, "as I have

Morgan's Bavarian-inspired designs for the buildings at Wyntoon blended perfectly into the pine forests that covered the surrounding land.

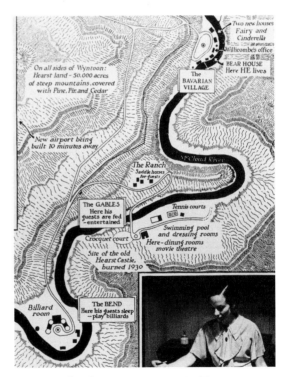

An article about Wyntoon in Fortune magazine included this map of the grounds, with Morgan's Bavarian Village shown in the upper-right-hand corner.

some stored in England and I am naturally going to attend to everything in connection with it; and all you have to do is just sit in it . . . which I know is very hard for you to do. Please let me try to help make the trip agreeable."

She left in November of 1934 and spent a chilly Christmas in Rome before embarking on the rest of her tour. When she returned in early April 1935, she began work on three houses for Wyntoon. They had a wistful style appropriate to the dim, forested landscape. Hearst named them Sleeping Beauty House, Cinderella House, and Bear House. Work continued through 1936, and eventually Wyntoon grew to include almost a dozen buildings.

Morgan approached her work as if she had never had her operation. Ignoring her loss of balance, she had several accidents on construction sites. Once at Wyntoon, she fell off a high scaffold, and according to her nephew, Morgan North, she slid two miles down a water flume before being rescued. She was drenched and badly bruised, but unfazed.

As Morgan's career drew to a close, new technology broadened architects' and engineers' horizons. The Golden Gate Bridge across San Francisco Bay opened in 1937, rendering obsolete the ferries Morgan had always used.

"My aunt had no fear of heights," Morgan's nephew recalled. "On the flimsiest of scaffolds or ladders she would be . . . climbing about on roofs. Many times she would be walking along and fall through a stairwell without stairs in it. Her head was a mass of scars and sutures. She had absolutely no fear of anything physical." But she was quite self-conscious. Because the botched operation had altered the lines of her face, Morgan attended even fewer public functions than she had before. An architect, she said, should never appear unsymmetrical.

As the economic depression deepened, the number of workers and gardeners at San Simeon shrank steadily. Hearst sent a series of telegrams to Morgan, gradually stopping all work at San Simeon, and then he asked for an inventory of the furnishings. According to a report Morgan prepared in 1937, when work stopped entirely, the construction on the Cuesta Encantada had cost $1,006,205.86. She would later estimate its total value, including furnishings and art, at $4,717,000. Yet Hearst's businesses and investments had by that time been severely affected by the Great Depression, and he could no longer afford such an extravagant lifestyle. In 1938 he left San Simeon.

Morgan's last major job for Hearst was the Medieval Museum. In 1931 Hearst had purchased parts of a Spanish monastery that stood in the mountains northeast of Madrid. It took six months just to crate the stones and bring them to California. Morgan and Hearst thought of rebuilding it at Wyntoon, but the architecture was inappropriate for the forested valleys there. The dozens of wood crates gathered dust in a warehouse until the summer of 1941, when Hearst offered to donate the monastery to the city of San Francisco. He imagined it as the core of a Museum of Medieval Arts, to be built on a small hill in Golden Gate Park. Morgan made a model of the reconstructed building as it would appear in its proposed location, and the city accepted the gift, storing the crates in a wooded area near the site. But funding for the project was never found, and over the years the crates were destroyed by fire. The stones, scattered and broken, lie there still.

The medieval project may have been thwarted by events taking place far away from San Francisco. World War II had broken out in Europe in 1939, and in 1941, after Japan attacked Pearl Harbor in Hawaii, the United States declared war on both Japan and Germany. The country concentrated on the war, and soon building materials such as lumber and copper were in short supply. The domestic construction industry suffered: Builders were unable to get what they needed, and many workers were drafted into military service. Morgan's practice dwindled accordingly.

Hearst's fortunes, however, improved during the war. In 1945 he returned to San Simeon, hoping to finish the upper floors of the north wing. Morgan, now 73, no longer had the energy for the job. She gave it to an assistant, George McClure. Then, in

In 1941 Morgan planned a medieval museum for San Francisco, but the stones originally intended for the project still lie in heaps in Golden Gate Park. Although some critics consider it her finest work, it was never built.

1947, Hearst's heart began to give out. In failing health, he abandoned San Simeon for good and moved to Los Angeles, where he died four years later.

When Morgan was 75, her memory began to fail. Nevertheless, she took on one of her last jobs, the remodeling of a home in Berkeley. She crossed the bay to examine the house and take the measurements she needed, but by the time she returned to San Francisco she had forgotten what the figures meant. It upset and frustrated her, and she realized that her days as an architect were almost through.

Morgan began to travel again. She made a five-month trip to South Amer-

ica at the end of 1947, and the following year she went to Europe, where she enjoyed taking local buses out to little country towns. She walked miles of narrow stone-paved streets, examining with an architect's eye the small houses and plain churches. Once, in the back country of Spain, she had another lapse of memory. Her mind went suddenly blank, and for a day she did not know where she was. Confused and alone, and still shy in her old age, she was unwilling to ask for help.

Morgan understood what was happening and did not like it. Both of her parents had lingered before they died, her mother ill and helpless, her father a

Her health and memory failing, Morgan (center) phased out her practice in the late 1940s and cruised to South America and Europe with her sister (left) and niece (right).

comatose invalid. Morgan wanted to go quickly. She told her niece Flora North that she hoped she would be at sea when she died.

In the summer of 1950, at the age of 78, Morgan finally closed her office. It had been 46 years since she had set up her drafting table in the Oakland carriage house, and she had accumulated a huge collection of drawings. In a postcard to each client, she asked if they wanted their drawings. Many of the owners had moved, and quite a number were dead, but Morgan sent plans to those who answered. She saved some of her design sketches and burned everything else. It took her most of a day, with the help of the building custodian,

During her final years, Morgan (seated at far left) turned to the North family for support and companionship. The great architect, who hated to bring attention to herself, was given a simple funeral.

to feed the rolled blueprints of a life-time into the furnace of the Merchants' Exchange Building.

Morgan did not get her wish to die quickly. In 1951, her memory waning still further, she had the first of a series of small strokes. As her condition worsened, she needed constant nursing. Her sister's family, the Norths—her closest friends in her last years—became to Morgan nothing more than a group of familiar faces, people that she knew. Her clear eyes grew cloudy, and the once-bright mind behind them slipped away. Finally, on February 2, 1957, Julia Morgan died. She was 85.

All her life Morgan had avoided publicity, and at her death her relatives honored her last wish, "Please give me a quick tuck-in with my own." Her carefully cultivated obscurity endured long after her death. At San Simeon, which became a California state park in the late 1950s, visitors can see an old home movie featuring William Randolph Hearst and his Hollywood guests. The film identifies a fleeting image of Morgan as Hearst's secretary, but now that Morgan's work has gained wide recognition, the guides at the castle correct this mistake.

Though she never sought fame, Morgan fought for the right to practice a traditionally male profession. By her dedication—and sheer talent—she won the respect of her colleagues and clients. Encouraged throughout her career by women, Morgan did much of her work for individual women and women's organizations. But she gave as much back to the women's community

as she gained from it, employing women architects, sponsoring women students, and paving the way for women who hoped to follow her into the field. Perhaps her greatest legacy, however, is a visual one.

"This great Californian, who designed not only San Simeon, but more than 700 other buildings in her long career..." wrote architecture critic Allan Temko, "deserves in American architecture at least as high a place as Mary Cassatt in American painting or Edith Wharton in American letters." Morgan herself might have denied playing so great a role in architectural history, but her achievements were indisputable. The citation that accompanied her honorary Berkeley degree in 1929 elegantly expressed Morgan's contributions:

> Julia Morgan, distinguished alumna of the University of California; artist and engineer; designer of simple dwellings and of stately homes, of great buildings nobly planned . . . architect in whose works harmony and admirable proportion bring pleasure to the eye and peace to the mind.

When she wrote to Pierre LeBrun after becoming the first woman admitted to the École des Beaux-Arts, Morgan had unwittingly predicted how she would earn such high praise. "It was no great thing," she wrote of her first victory, "but it has taken quite a little effort . . . a mixture of dislike of giving up some thing attempted and the sense of its being a sort of test . . . made it seem a thing that had to be won." And win she did.

FURTHER READING

Aidala, Thomas. *Hearst Castle, San Simeon.* New York: Hudson Hills Press, 1981.

Beach, John. *Architectural Drawings by Julia Morgan: Beaux-Arts Assignments and Other Buildings.* Oakland: The Oakland Museum Art Department, 1976.

Boutelle, Sara Holmes. *Julia Morgan.* New York: Abbeville Press, 1988.

Burchard, John, and Albert Bush-Brown. *The Architecture of America: A Social and Cultural History.* Boston: Little, Brown, 1961.

Coffman, Taylor. *Hearst Castle, The Story of William Randolph Hearst and San Simeon.* Santa Barbara, CA: Sequoia Communications, 1985.

Hunt, James D. *A Companion to California.* New York: Oxford University Press, 1978.

————. *Julia Morgan, Architect.* Berkeley, CA: Berkeley Architectural Heritage Association, 1986.

Longstreth, Richard. *On the Edge of the World: Four Architects in San Francisco at the Turn of the Century.* Cambridge: MIT Press, 1983.

Richey, Elinor. *Eminent Women of the West.* Berkeley: Howell-North Books, 1975.

Riess, Suzanne B., ed. *The Julia Morgan Architectural History Project: The Work of Walter Steilberg and Julia Morgan* (vol. 1) and *Julia Morgan, Her Office and A House* (vol 2). Bancroft Library, University of California Regional Oral History Office, Berkeley: The Regents of The University of California, 1976.

CHRONOLOGY

Jan. 28, 1872	Julia Morgan born in San Francisco
1873	Moves to Oakland
1890	Graduates from Oakland High School; enters the University of California at Berkeley
1894	Graduates from University of California at Berkeley with a B.S. in civil engineering
1895	Works and studies with Bernard Maybeck
1896	Travels to Paris
1898	Becomes first woman accepted to the architecture program at the École des Beaux-Arts
1901	Receives her certificate in architecture from the École des Beaux-Arts
1902	Returns home; works for John Galen Howard
1903	Opens own architecture practice
1904	Earns architect's license from State of California; designs El Campanil at Mills College
1906	San Francisco earthquake; Morgan begins reconstruction of Fairmont Hotel
1909	Designs home for Emma and Hart North
1910	Builds St. John's Presbyterian Church in Berkeley
1912	Draws site plan for YWCA camp in Asilomar, California
1913	Designs Oakland YWCA
1917	Plans two Hostess Houses for World War I soldiers
1919	Meets William Randolph Hearst; starts construction of San Simeon
1922	Designs Hollywood Studio Club
1924	Morgan's father dies
1925	Designs Phoebe Apperson Hearst Memorial Gymnasium for Women with Bernard Maybeck
1927	Completes the Casa Grande at San Simeon
1929	Serves as architect for Principia College, St. Louis, with Maybeck; receives honorary Doctor of Laws degree from University of California at Berkeley; mother dies
1932	Morgan begins work on San Francisco YWCA; undergoes surgery for ear infection
1933	Plans Bavarian-style cottages for Wyntoon
1936	Begins construction on Wyntoon houses
1937	On Hearst's orders, stops work at San Simeon
1941	Morgan plans reconstruction of medieval Spanish monastery
1950	Closes office
Feb. 2, 1957	Dies at the age of 85

INDEX

PICTURE CREDITS

Bancroft Library, University of California, Berkeley, pp. 15, 36, 38, 39, 40, 50, 51, 67, 89; Bettmann, pp. 14, 16, 30, 31, 41, 52, 55, 62, 70, 94, 100; Special Collections, California Polytechnic State University, frontispiece, pp. 12, 19, 20, 21, 22, 25, 26–27, 28, 37, 42, 44, 48, 53, 54, 56, 57, 58, 60, 71, 64–65, 66, 74, 75, 76, 78, 80, 81, 82, 84, 85, 86, 88, 90, 93, 94, 95, 96, 98, 102, 103, 104; Collection Viollet, Paris, p. 34; College of Environmental Design, University of California, Berkeley, pp. 46, 59; Culver Pictures, pp. 32–33, 72; Courtesy of *Fortune* Magazine, p. 99; Marilyn Blaisdell Collection, p. 17; National Board YWCA Archives, pp. 63, 68, 69, 92; The New York Historical Society, p. 24; San Francisco Public Library, p. 29; Hearst San Simeon State Historical Monument, pp. 77, 79, 99

Cary James was born in Virginia and graduated from the College of William and Mary. He studied architecture at the University of California at Berkeley and currently works as an architect in the San Francisco Bay area. His previous works include *The Imperial Hotel: Frank Lloyd Wright and the Architecture of Unity*.

❖   ❖   ❖

Matina S. Horner is president of Radcliffe College and associate professor of psychology and social relations at Harvard University. She is best known for her studies of women's motivation, achievement, and personality development. Dr. Horner serves on several national boards and advisory councils, including those of the National Science Foundation, Time Inc., and the Women's Research and Education Institute. She earned her B.A. from Bryn Mawr College and Ph.D. from the University of Michigan, and holds honorary degrees from many colleges and universities, including Mount Holyoke, Smith, Tufts, and the University of Pennsylvania.